YOUR OFFICIAL GUIDE ON HOW TO
DOMINATE FANTASY FOOTBALL
BY RANDY GIMINEZ

D1026060

HOMEPAGE
PUBLISHING L.L.P.

YOUR OFFICIAL GUIDE ON HOW TO
DOMINATE FANTASY FOOTBALL

Author: Randy Giminez

Web site design: Chris Giminez, Cyber-Scriber Web Site Design, www.cyber-scriber.com

Web site graphic design, book design: Travis Williams, Rivet Creative, www.rivetcreative.com

Publisher: HomePage Publishing, LLP, Blue Springs, MO

Trademark acknowledgements: All trademarks are the property of their re-spective owners. The companies mentioned in this book in no way endorse the contents of this book, nor have they participated in the publication of this book. All product illustrations, name and logos are trademarks of their respective manufacturers. All terms in this book that are known or suspect-ed to be trademarks or service marks have been indicated as such, are should be assumed as such. Use of an illustration, term, or logo in this book should not be regarded as affecting the ability of any trademark or service mark.

Library of Congress Control Number: 2006924953
ISBN - 13: 978-0-9779105-0-2
ISBN – 10: 0-9779105-0-4

Printed in the U.S.A

Acknowledgements

When it became evident at the end of the fantasy football season that my strategies were going to pay off in winning championship games, I began toying with the idea of putting those strategies into a book. My biggest obstacle was the fact that I'm not a writer. I'm much more comfortable with numbers than words. But, never one to back down from a hurdle, I plunged on into the publishing world. Sometimes it's best to be oblivious of the difficulties ahead in the path you've chosen or you won't experience the deep satisfaction of attaining a goal.

Needless to say, I wouldn't have accomplished this goal without the encouragement, suggestions, and cooperation of others. On the literary side, I'd like to thank Mariah Andrews for her copyediting magic. When I was beginning to feel bogged down by the manuscript, she appeared and rescued it. As I mentioned before, Mariah, I bow to your greatness.

I'd like to thank my parents, Tino and Dessa Giminez. Without you this book would not be possible, because about 40 years ago you planted the seed of "thinking out of the box".

Thank you, Luster and Bonnie Williams, my in-laws and bowlers extraordinaire for your supportive encouragement. I've never regretted moving close to you.

To my three children, Josh, Saul, and Rachael, thanks for your unique personalities to keep me from boredom.

To my Heroes, who helped me spread my thoughts and ideas for the book over the World Wide Web in style:

To Travis Williams, graphic artist, illustrator, ad/web designer and brother-in-law, I owe much gratitude. Your caviar abilities pushed my hamburger style to another level.

To my brother, Chris Giminez, I am constantly amazed at your web design genius. Thank you for your relentless labor on this web site. The man behind our web site engine.

To my wife, Karla, without your neverending support this project had no chance. Words cannot fully express what having you stand by my side daily means to me. However, I do wish to say thank you...for teaching me the real meaning of life.

To All,
Thank you for being in my life.

(continued)

(continued)

INTRODUCTION:
Welcome to Dominate Fantasy Football

WHAT YOU WILL LEARN:

1. **How to use this book**
2. **An introduction to scoring**
3. **The author's experience**

Overview

Welcome to the fantasy football world. There are estimated to be 15 million (and growing) players who enjoy the game of fantasy football. That translates to about one in 20 people across the U.S. of A. Many may play for fun or for money, but all have one objective – to win the championship game. Most fantasy football leagues contain 12 players, such as yourself. Throughout this book, you'll be known as a coach. Unfortunately, for every winner, there will be eleven losing coaches. This book is designed to show you what it takes to dominate – to be that one championship winner at the end of the season. I am very happy to share it with you.

1.1 - HOW TO USE THIS BOOK

Your fantasy football magazines are devised to give you loads of projections and stats to kick start your fantasy football thinking at the beginning of the year. On the web, there are many sites to help you when choosing and managing your particular players on a weekly basis.

Both the magazines and web sites do their job admirably. However, neither one is designed to fully explain the overall strategies to implement throughout the entire season. To truly grasp the complexities of playing the game to win, you need an in-depth resource. This book is that re-source, and you'll find it's like no other book ever written on the subject of fantasy football.

Whether you're new to the fantasy football game or an experienced play-er, you'll find more than a hundred strategies, tips and tidbits expressly designed to take your game to the next level. Many of the strategies will be revolutionary, and you'll need to keep an open mind to get the most out of this book.

Note to self...take notes.

Over 100 tactics are too many for any one person to absorb. You are en-couraged to read this book with a pencil in one hand and a highlighter in the other. Note-taking is a must. Write notes on the pages provided in back of this book on the points you're going to use and how you plan to use them. Also, make notes on the points with which you disagree and the reasons why. After you finish reading the book, go back and reread those disagreements to see if they now make more sense. Use your high-lighter frequently to help locate passages you may need to refer to during the season. The end of this book has a section for your diary (more about your diary in section 8.2). Don't worry, we didn't color it in pink or put bows around this section, but it is an important part of learning how to play fantasy football once the season begins. Just after the diary section is one page to write down your page numbers for reference keys. To get the most out of this book, use it correctly and keep it as a reference guide through the entire season.

Throughout the book, you'll notice some text that is bolded and some text italicized. The bolded text is to bring attention to the point intended. The italicized texts are my personal experiences and/or dated to a previous year.

Fantasy football, played correctly and played to win, is 90 % tactical (most fantasy football coaches do not understand this). The knowledge shared in this book is based on 10 years of experience and from the statistics from Chapter 10. Chapter 10 breaks down the numbers and entertains the "why" of the strategies revealed in this book. This is based on analysis of 21 of my leagues and over 3,500 games played in 2005. There will be many references in the book to Chapter 10.

1.2 - REFERENCE LEAGUE

This is very important. This entire book has been written for the coach who plays in a league that drafts a roster of 14 or less players and uses the performance scoring system. Millions of fantasy football players will fit this book to a "T," however, you must know your own league's parameters to make adjustments from the book's strategies. Even if your league is set up differently, you'll find that many of the strategies still work for you. But it's up to you to find the modifications needed for your league or you need to play in a standard league.

Dominate Fantasy Football uses the following stats as a guide throughout the book. This constitutes my version of the standard league setup and scoring.

The draft is 14 players and your weekly starters consist of 8 players (1 QB, 2 RB, 2 WR, 1 TE, 1 K, 1 D)

Waiver wire is unlimited. Scoring is head-to-head. Playoffs are Week 15 and championship game is Week 16 of the NFL season. Draft is serpentine and is live online.

Main scoring is:

Field goals – 3 pts. plus 2 pts. if longer than 50 yards
Fumble lost – 2 pts.
Passing, receiving, rushing TD – all are 6 pts.
Passing yards – 1 pt. for every 25 yards
Rushing and receiving yards – 1 pt. for every 10 yards
Extra point – 1 pt.

For Defense (higher than many leagues):

Defensive fumble recovered – 2 pts.
TD scored by defense or special teams – 6 pts.
Interception – 2 pts.
Sack – 1 pt.
Safety – 2 pts.
Points scored against – 8 to 0 pts. on a sliding scale
Yards allowed against – 12 to 0 on a sliding scale

1.3 - MY FANTASY FOOTBALL EXPERIENCE

I have played since the late '80s, before the Internet really took off. My early years were played for fun and bragging rights between myself, my father, Tino, my brother, Chris, and my son, Saul. Later years, we played on the ESPN site with standard leagues.

In 2004, I wanted to expand my horizons and perhaps make some money for my time. My research led me to CBS Sportsline™, which I believe runs a very nice game.

That year, I purchased six leagues and made the playoffs in four of the leagues. Out of the four playoffs, I won the championship in one league. I thought my strategies were pretty sound, but I realized I was not ready to win the big games when it counted.

I began a more in-depth research of the game. I found that playing fantasy football and winning fantasy football are two totally different things. With this understanding, I changed many of my old ideas. I felt sure of my abilities, but I needed to put my money where my mouth was.

Tastes like chicken.

In 2005, I purchased 21 teams. I made the playoffs in 16 (76%). In the first playoff week, I won 14 out of 16 (87%). And, in the championship game, the one that counted, I won 12 out of 14 (86 %).

My 85% + win factor in the playoff and championship rounds were dominating. In winning the 12 championships, I cashed a check from CBS Sportsline for $32,500.

Also in 2005, I played in three ESPN leagues and won the championship in all three.

Now that is one dominating football season. See the chart on the next page for more details.

WARNING: All of the information is this book is based on a standard league roster and performance scoring. If you play in a non-standard league, it is your responsibility to understand how any or all of the strategies can impact your team.

SportsLine is a registered service mark of SportsLine.com, Inc. All other brand names mentioned in this book are trade- or service marks of their respective companies.

1.4 - MY LEAGUES AND TEAMS FOR 2005:

$1,600.00   **CBS LEAGUE - CONTENDERS**
ATOMIZERS - Won Championship by 60 Pts.

CBS LEAGUE - LABOR DAY CELEBRATION
CHEESEHEADS - Scored 2nd Highest League Pts.
(Did not make the playoffs.)

CBS LEAGUE - WALK THE TALK
DAFFY - Improved Scoring Average from 68.7 to 109.5 Pts.
(Just missed making the playoffs.)

$3,500.00   **CBS LEAGUE- VIP FOOTBALL**
GERONIMO - Won Championship by 40 Pts.

$1,600.00   **CBS LEAGUE - BLACK AND BLUE DIVISION**
GOLD STARS - Won Championship by 21 Pts.

$3,500.00   **CBS LEAGUE - HORSE TRADERS WANTED**
HANG EM HIGH - Won Championship by 47 Pts.

CBS LEAGUE - THE GRIDIRON CLASSIC
HELLCAT COOL - Lost in the Championship Game

$3,500.00   **CBS LEAGUE - LONELY HEARTS CLUB BAND**
JOKER - Won Championship by 40 Pts.

CBS LEAGUE - SURVIVOR
LIONHEART - Lost Playoff Game by 1 Pt.

$3,500.00   **CBS LEAGUE - WHO HAS THEIR SHI? TOGETHER**
LOTTA BULL - Won Championship by 52 Pts.

$1,600.00   **CBS LEAGUE - DOUBLE DOWN**
LUPAS - Won Championship by 18 Pts.

$1,600.00   **CBS LEAGUE - COLONEL MUSTARDS MISFITS**
MEXICAN MUDCATS - Won Championship by 35 Pts.

CBS LEAGUE - DEAL AND PLAY
NEMO - Could Not Get It Going in Any Phase
(Did not make the playoffs.)

CBS LEAGUE - FOR THE REAL FAN
PISTOLA PETE - Lost in the Championship Game

$3,500.00   ### CBS LEAGUE - MEN ARE FROM MARS
POOH - Won Championship by 18 Pts.

CBS LEAGUE - PRIME TIME FOOTBALL
RACHAEL'S ROBINS - 4th Highest League Pts.
(Did not make the playoffs.)

CBS LEAGUE - WEST COAST FOOTBALL FANATICS
RAMBLIN MAN - Lost Playoff by 4 Pts.

$3,500.00   ### CBS LEAGUE - BS
ROCKET MAN - Won Championship by 71 Pts.

$3,500.00   ### CBS LEAGUE - NFL 2KV
TWEETY - Won Championship by 7 Pts.

CBS LEAGUE - THE BIG DAWGS
WANNA BEES - Scored 2nd Highest League Pts.
(Did not make the playoffs.)

$1,600.00   ### CBS LEAGUE - THE MONEY SHOT
ZERO ZIPPOS - Won Championship by 16 Pts.

BANNER   ### ESPN LEAGUE - NEW JERSEY VIKINGS FAN
TRIFECTA MAN - Won Championship by 70 Pts.

BANNER   ### ESPN LEAGUE - VIKINGS ROCK
WANNA BEES - Won Championship by 85 Pts.

BANNER   ### ESPN LEAGUE - BLEDSOE FANS ONLY
LEAPIN LIZARDS - Won Championship by 42 Pts.

CHAPTER 1 - INTRODUCTION

CHAPTER 2

WHAT YOU WILL LEARN:

1. How to get started
2. How to identify your opponents
4. What kinds of leagues are out there
5. Terms used in Fantasy Football and throughout this book

Overview

Fantasy football was born on a rainy October night in 1962, in a hotel room in New York by the late Wilford "Bill" Winkerenbach and two friends, Bill Tunnell and Scotty Stirling. They were just as passionate about the game then as we are today. Although the passion still remains, the game has grown tremendously and now permeates the Internet world.

Why is fantasy football the most popular of all fantasy sports? The most obvious reason is the game is played once a week and, in most cases, as a head-to-head competition. Most other fantasy sports don't have this luxury. A coach has all week to plan, scheme, talk smack or whatever passionate pursuit of the game fulfills his or her needs.

Another reason could be because it's one of least expensive hobbies around. For a few dollars and a little time, you own NFL players (in name only). From beginners to experts, we're all given an opportunity to be the coach/general manager/owner of our own team. You can name the team whatever your little heart desires. Fantasy football allows fans to take an active, personal role in professional football, thereby increasing the enjoyment of the game.

2.1 - HOW TO PLAY

There's a lot to do before you actually start to play. First, you must join a fantasy football league. There are hundreds of leagues from which to choose, with more coming online every year. In selecting a league, you are faced with these choices:

1. The type of opponent
2. The type of rules
3. The type of prize

Out of the hundreds of leagues out there, you will find three main contest sites:

1. Yahoo! - the largest of the sites, it's for beginners and free.
2. ESPN - the cable channel's site is excellent, offering a low-cost entry and low prize values.
3. CBS Sportsline - a site with low-to-middle entry cost and low-to-high prize money.

There are many other very reputable games, though one of the problems (if you see it as a problem) is the larger sites contests are standardized, while some smaller sites leagues can be more flexible.

If you want to play for big money, check out: www.UFFLive.com, www.FantasyVIPs.com, www.WCOFF.com and www.FantasyFootball Championship.com, just to name a few. They pay upwards of 200k for the championship prize.

To avoid confusion, play in leagues with the same type of scoring and similar rules.

The best way to find different leagues is not through the search engines, but via your assistant coaches (see section 9.6). These sites are linked to hundreds of fantasy football contest sites.

Once you've joined a league, the next big step is to draft your players. A standard league consists of 12 "owners" or "coaches," and each of you will create your own unique roster by drafting talent from the actual NFL teams. You'll select a roster of between 14 and 20 NFL players (depending on the rules).

Do not expect to win the first year. Play for a year, get to know the rules and tendencies of your league and learn from it. You should have all the experience you need to dominate the next year.

After the draft, the real fun begins and you finally get to play! Just like in the NFL, you'll go head-to-head with a different team, each and every week.

You, as coach, will choose a starting lineup each week. This typically consists of 1 QB, 2 RB, 2 WR, 1 TE, 1 K, AND 1 D (Defense)

The starting lineups for each team will accumulate points which are based on the actual performance of the NFL Players. The team with the most points is credited for the win.

Once you complete your regular weekly schedule, which is most likely in Weeks 13 or 14, you then can qualify for the playoffs. Generally, the top one or two teams per division will make the playoffs which last one to two weeks. The winners advance, while the losers bow out, which leads to Week 16 and the championship. The championship game involves the final two teams battling it out to claim the prize – and bragging rights for the year. All leagues distribute different rewards. Some offer prize money, while others may offer a trophy or a T-shirt, but the bottom line of the game is to have fun.

Here fishy, fishy.

2.2 - WHO WILL YOU PLAY AGAINST?

In most online leagues, you won't know who your opponent is. In fact, he or she may live clear across the United States. You can, however, recognize your opponent's skill level by his or her actions. To help you do this, I've grouped the types of fantasy football coaches/owners into four categories: fish, dolphins, sharks and whales. Here is what to expect from each type of player category:

Fish/Beginner
Your typical fish plays for the pure fun of the game; winning is secondary. He is always looking for the trade and, much of the time, only for the sake of doing a trade. His main source of knowledge is the fantasy football magazines. Only around 20 percent of players annually can be categorized as fish, as you are only a beginner for a short time. You either move up or quit playing.

How to Identify a Fish:

1. He routinely wants a QB in the first round.
2. Homerism is his middle name. (See section 7.4)
3. He doesn't understand that you always start your studs.
4. He doesn't know the league's scoring rules.
5. He drafts a backup kicker.
6. He relies on out-of-date magazines for his draft choices.
7. He drafts handcuffs instead of value.
8. He gives up on good players too early in the season.
9. He doesn't keep informed on injuries.
10. He will win only when lady luck smiles on him.

If you are a fish, you probably need to read this book more than once.

Dolphins/Intermediate

Dolphins will generally not make the same mistakes as a fish, as they tend to try to learn more with each year. This coach puts in more time than the fish and usually sees better results. He gets his information from the contest site and his fantasy football magazines. This is your biggest group by far. Their mistakes are plentiful, but not as deadly.

How to Identify a Dolphin:

1. He drinks too much on draft day.
2. He favors name recognition over production
3. He falls for the rookie hype.
4. He follows a stud RB theory too strictly.
5. He takes last year's stats strictly at face value.
6. He drafts with his heart.
7. He hangs on to poor players too long.
8. He carries third-rate players on his roster.
9. He doesn't prepare properly for the draft.
10. He reaches for sleepers on draft day.
11. He ignores working the waiver wire.
12. He doesn't understand the importance of coaching changes.
13. He gets his information only from his league's web site.

14. He ignores the NFL team philosophy.
15. He will win 10 percent of the leagues he enters.

If you see yourself here, this book was written just for you. It will take your game to the next level very quickly.

Sharks/Experts

These coaches will work all the angles, like to talk smack, and put in so much time even they believe their own hype. Their biggest attribute is not making mistakes and understanding that this is a marathon, not a sprint. He knows stats the best and uses multiple web sites for his information. The top 15 percent of the players today fit the mold of a shark.

How to Identify a Shark:

1. He still fears the impact of the NFL bye week.
2. He prepares for the draft by tiering his players.
3. He uses the VBD as a drafting technique.
4. He knows that formulas are only good if they fit your league's scoring.
5. He studies the rules and then studies them again.
6. He realizes that a good NFL player may not be a good fantasy football player.
7. He won't drop a good player after a couple of bad games.
8. He knows the real draft starts in Round 4.
9. He likes to work the two-fers.
10. He compares every player to the player himself – with the upside risk vs. the downside risk.
11. He considers a player's health and age for each position.
12. He pays for more than two web sites to keep him abreast new information throughout the season.
13. He searches his computer for information at least once a day.
14. He loves to talk smack.
15. He understands the difference between the NFL game and the fantasy football game.
16. Will win 20 to 25 percent of the leagues he enters.

Most sharks won't benefit greatly from this book. They would rather argue than open their minds, if only because they have tasted the champ ionship before.

Whales/Top of the Food Chain

The whale understands the true nature of the game and that the strategies go beyond the players in the NFL game. He gets his information from multiple web sites and checks his information several times a day, ready to scoop his competition. A whale is a very rare find – he's in the top one percent of all players. You may never play against a whale in your entire fantasy football "career" but, if you do, you may never know it.

How to Identify a Whale:

1. He loves the bye week for all of its advantages.
2. He continually works to improve his team.
3. He builds his team to get "hot" at the right time.
4. He checks his advice sites at least three times a day for the very latest information.
5. He has a disciplined plan from the beginning and follows it to a "T."
6. He understands how the game is really to be played.
7. He will win over 50 percent, and maybe up to 75 percent, of leagues he enters, depending on his competition.

Whales will love this book, as they will always be on the lookout for one or two new ideas.

Do you see yourself in a category? Maybe you are a 'tweener – some of one category and also some of another. After reading this book, you will certainly move up. While I may have classified the typical player, in fantasy football, everyone maintains expert status *in their own minds*.

2.3 - CHOICES IN LEAGUE SELECTION

Novice = (●)   Expert = (●)(●)(●)

Amateur = (●)(●)   Master = (●)(●)(●)(●)

* indicates CBS Sportsline®, the league in which this book is based.

Draft Type

1.* Serpentine (●) – standard; the draft "snakes" (see Chapter 5)
2. Auction (●)(●)(●) – salary cap; coaches acquire players by bidding on them like an auction; considered more fair, but very difficult

Draft Method

1. Auto-pick (●) – the computer makes the picks, based on your earlier chosen preferences
2.* Online (●)(●) – live; meet on the Internet at a specified time
3. At the site (●)(●) - live draft; coaches are assembled in one room to draft players in the presence of each another

Draft Time – Time you are given to make each selection

1. 45 seconds (●)(●)(●) – a bit fast
2.* 90 seconds (●) – Much better, but the overall draft lasts longer

Roster Size

1. 14 players (●) – fairly standard
2. 16 players (●)(●)
3. 18 players (●)(●)(●) – higher numbers mean fewer players left in the player pool, which translates to the actual draft being more important in your overall strategy
4. 20 players (●)(●)(●)
5. 24 players (●)(●)(●)(●)
6. 26 players (●)(●)(●)(●)

Lineups Submitted (Starters) – Basic roster must be considered.

1.* Standard (●) – 1 QB, 2 RB, 2 WR, 1 TE, 1 K, 1 D
2. Three wide receivers (●)(●) – the same as #1 with 3 WR

3. Flex RB, WR, TE (⬤⬤⬤) – the same as #1 with a 9th player, which could be either a RB, WR, TE; much more strategy needed here
4. IDP (⬤⬤⬤⬤) (Individual Defensive Players) – the same as #1 plus an IDP; very difficult dimension to the game

League Size
1. 8 owners (⬤) – studs galore for everyone
2. 10 owners (⬤)
3.* 12 owners (⬤) – standard, as seems to be just right for most fantasy football coaches
4. 14 owners (⬤⬤⬤) – this many owners depletes the free agent pool very quickly

Division Size
1.* 4 team division (⬤) – 12 teams /3 divisions are standard
2. 6 team division (⬤⬤)

Scoring
1. Standard/Basic (⬤⬤⬤) – TD only
2.* Performance (⬤) – a scoring system that awards fantasy points for touchdowns and yardage
3. Modified (⬤⬤) – a good example is a point per catch plus the #2 performance from above, which would put more of a premium on the WR group. Leagues can do any scoring modifications within the starting positions they wish.
   a. Bonus – points given for more extraordinary plays or for full game stats. Examples: TD's for more than 50 yards receive a bonus, or a RB who reaches 100 yards for a game will receive a bonus. Also used with #2 above.
   b. Fractional Points – carries the scoring to two decimal spots; what would be 85 points in a performance league, will be 87.32 points with fractional scoring format. This reduces the likelihood of a tie, while also receiving every ounce of a player's performance in your score.

Leagues

1.* Head-to-Head (◉) – standard play, matches the NFL format
2. Experts (◉◉◉) – on paper, you play every team in your league every week. Much harder to strategize, as you cannot prepare for just one team. This type of league tries to eliminate the factor of luck when naming its champion.
3.* Re-draft (◉) – league does not allow managers to carry players over from season-to-season; new team is drafted each year
4. Keeper (◉◉◉) – some of the players are retained between seasons
5. Private – you must be invited to play in, usually a group of friends
6. Public – league that invites anyone to play as opposed to private

Trades

1.* Limited (◉) – won't allow trades later in the season to lessen the possibility of collusion
2. Unlimited (◉) – no restrictions if you find a trading partner.
3. None (◉◉) – very difficult, but no collusion between players.

Waiver and Free Agents

1. Anytime (◉◉) – even during the actual NFL games; no lock down period; players go to the swiftest or whoever "lives" next to their computer 24 hours a day
2.* Worst-to-First (◉) – allows coaches with the worst records the first choice on picking up the best available player from the player pool.
3. Bidding (◉◉◉) – every coach is given a set amount of "play" dollars to spend throughout the year on the free agents. When the money is gone, the coach cannot use the bidding system any longer.
4. Blind bidding (◉◉◉◉) – allows coaches to bid with "play" money for the free agents on the waiver wire. Blind means

coaches must make their bids without any knowledge of what the other coaches are doing.

5. Charge for "all" roster changes (ongoing fees) (▣)(▣) – ouch, unless you have deep pockets, maybe you can buy your way to a championship

You can mix and match these options, as I am sure there is a league that will have one of each category.

As you search out the leagues, find one (or more) that fits you and join up. One thing to keep in mind is never select a league that has the championship game on Week 17 (see Chapter 8). In addition to joining your league(s), there are some other very exciting and different fantasy football games to play – for money and for free. Peek at section 9.6 for more on this.

This league fits like a glove.

2.4 - FANTASY FOOTBALL TERMINOLOGY

ADP – Average Draft Position – this indicates when a player is likely to be drafted. For instance, 3.04 means a player is likely to be drafted in the third round with the fourth pick.

Assistant Manager – (DFF term) The advice web site used to help a coach make decisions about his team.

Bench player – A player who is not in your starting lineup for the week.

'Bility – (DFF term) A special word combining flexibility and adjustability for power to dominate.

Bust – A fantasy football player who significantly underperforms his projection.

Bye Trader – (DFF term) A coach who will specialize in trades made during the Bye Season (Weeks 3 -9).

Bye Week – The one week all NFL teams get during the regular season. The fantasy team does not receive a bye during the regular season; however, your individual players will all have bye weeks.

Cheatsheet – A spreadsheet you create with player rankings and projections. You will use this sheet during the draft.

Coach/Manager/Owner – This would be you, the person responsible for paying league entry fees, drafting players, submitting weekly lineups, offering trades, working the free agency system, and much more.

Commissioner – The person who is responsible for the enforcement of the league's rules and is in charge of judging the fairness of situations that may arise between coaches during the year. His voice his final.

DFF – Dominate Fantasy Football.

Doubtful – A term used by the NFL that flags a particular player as having a 25 percent chance to play in this week's game.

FFRV – (DFF term) Fantasy Football Real Value – A subjective value put on a NFL player by a coach for the good of his team and has little relation to the current rankings.

Free agent – A player who is in the player pool and is available for any coach to pickup.

Handcuff – To pick the NFL backup to your starting fantasy player, usually your RB position.

Hole – (DFF term) The numbered position that a coach will draft from.

Homerism – (DFF term) Wanting a particular NFL player on your team only because the player plays for your favorite NFL team.

Match Up – Looking at the team your player(s) are going up against. You prefer to be playing against weak NFL teams for a successful match up.

Mock Draft – A pretend draft used to hone your drafting skills. Coaches practice drafting players.

Player Pool – Where to find any NFL players who are not currently on a roster.

Preferred Players – A list of NFL players a coach prefers to be on his roster.

Probable – A term used by the NFL that flags a particular player as having a 75 percent chance to play in this week's game.

Projection – The predicted fantasy points a player is going to score.

Questionable – A term used by the NFL that flags a particular player as having a 50 percent chance to play in this week's game.

RBBC – Running Back By Committee – a situation which involves two RBs on one NFL team that share the carries for the team. This is a situation to avoid in fantasy football, as the running back would have fewer opportunities to score points.

Sleeper – A player believed to have more potential than his current ranking would indicate.

Spotter – (DFF term) The weakest player on your roster who is identified early, so that a coach may drop him without hesitation.

Stud – A top-rated player.

Tax Planning FF Style – (DFF term) Planning ahead for tax advantages for fantasy football income.

Tiering – An advanced method of grouping like players together for the purpose of helping your overall draft.

Two-Fer – (DFF term) One action that has two benefits.

VBD – Value Based Drafting – used by most experts in working the draft. This method finds the best available player with a mathematical formula. It also gives you another option for every pick to work within your own draft strategy.

Veto – Used by the commissioner or coaches to reject a trade offer between two teams.

Waiver Wire – A system that governs how coaches are able to pick up their free agent choices.

Wart – (DFF term) A player on a roster who is not pulling his own weight for the team.

CHAPTER 3

SETTING THE BAR:
Play to Win

WHAT YOU WILL LEARN:
1. The role of the coach
2. What it takes to win
3. Why history is of utmost importance
4. What your main focus needs to be throughout the season
5. How many wins you need to make the playoffs
6. What you need to score in the championship game to dominate

Overview

Many fantasy football coaches play just for the fun involved, but doesn't winning increase the fun? To win consistently, you must understand the game for what it is. That's what this chapter is all about – playing the game to win. Throughout this book, I will give you tips to remain focused on the championship game and offer lessons to implement strategies and attain your goal. After you learn these lessons, you can still have fun with the individual players and root for your favorites.

3.1 - AM I READY TO DOMINATE?

Let's have a one-question test. I hope you pass!

What do you want to say to yourself when the draft is over?
A. I got my favorite stud and love my team.
B. I am loaded.
C. This should impress my friends, spouse and family members.
D. It looks like I have a very competitive team.
E. I'm set up to win the championship game.

If you picked A, B, C or D, you are like the majority of coaches after their draft. If you've played before, think back to last year. What were your thoughts about the players you coveted and the team you wanted to start the NFL season? It's natural to want your favorite players and you just may walk into a championship with them, but the odds are against you. That is what this book is all about — the odds. They need to be stacked in your favor. You need to look under every rock and in every crevice to find any strategy, advantage or tip that will put the odds overwhelmingly on your side. If you do not, you will have a rerun. A rerun is the same old show as last season and, for you, it will be the same old result.

Don't rewind the rerun season!

If your answer is E, congratulations! You have just taken the first step toward dominating. **Like a head coach in the NFL, you must be focused 100 percent of the time on the championship game.** At the beginning of each year, every NFL team starts out with a record of 0-0 and all have one objective — to win the Super Bowl. Every collective breath they take has that goal in mind.

Build your team from the very beginning to play the strongest game possible in the championship round. The rest of the book is based on this strategy.

In fantasy football, your Super Bowl is the championship game in Week 16. But many of your fellow coaches believe the championship for fantasy football begins at the draft. After you read this chapter, you will know better. You will know that winning the championship needs to be your focus at every stage in the game. You will know that winning is not about getting the best "stud" players, but the best overall team. And I will help you know what you need to focus on to win at the championship level.

3.2 - WHAT IS THE ROLE OF THE COACH?

In the NFL, when two teams square off against each other, they are planning an all-out war to win the game. Who we see and root for or against are the players who take the field. But those players are only pawns used by the coach of the team. In actuality, it is one coach pitted against another. The coach has all the strategies and calls all the plays. The coach never looks at one play to make a game or at one game to make the season. He is always looking at the big picture – how to build a championship team.

In fantasy football, as in the NFL, it is one coach pitted against another. The coach calls all the strategies and all the plays. The players are only there to keep score.

In fantasy football, you, too, will always need to focus on building a championship team. Each piece of information you obtain, no matter where you get it from, must be filtered through a question: "How can I turn this information into a true advantage for my team?" This shift in perspective, from individual players and games to strategies and goals, is essential to your success.

Goal-driven coaches act, not react. Be a goal-driven coach!

Another one of your duties as a coach is to read the league rules very carefully and look between the lines to find any benefit for your team. Locating and implementing strategies to take advantage of the rules is one of the most important roles of the coach. The rules are there to treat everyone the same and are in the interest of fairness. Don't collude or cheat in any way, but do find the advantages. Many leagues have different rules and it is up to you to find a league that fit the strategies you will be implementing. Even the smallest advantage can help. That is exactly what the NFL coaches do when they analyze game films.

The most successful coaches are the best-informed coaches.

What is an advantage? Let's look at an example from the NFL. An NFL team wants to throw a bomb. Where do they throw, in the middle of the field or the sidelines? They prefer to throw bombs down the sidelines. Why? Because 1). the receiver cannot be covered on both sides, 2). if the ball is overthrown, it will be out of bounds and 3). if the receiver catches the ball and subsequently fumbles, it will possibly roll out of bounds. Those are advantages to throwing down the sideline. Only a fool will play a team straight up, "mano vs mano."

A coach has a responsibility to search for every advantage for the benefit of his team.

There are actually more advantages in fantasy football as you are not restricted to on-field play calling. Remember, you are playing a different game.

An advantage in fantasy football could be as simple as choosing which league to play. You could play in a division with six teams or a division with four teams. The division winner usually makes the playoffs; therefore, why not play with the smaller division and have less competition? Only a fool plays "mano vs. mano".

3.3 - OUTSMART. OUT HUSTLE. OUTWORK.

When you're competing against an opponent, there are two axioms you need to put on your side: 1). Work smarter and 2). put in more time than your opponent. I will show you how to work smarter, but the second part is up you. The average fantasy football player puts about four hours a week into his or her leagues. You need to be willing to work harder than your opponents to give you a huge advantage.

**Hard work now makes winning easier, and
easy work now makes winning harder.**

You only have to outsmart, out hustle, and outwork 11 other coaches. It really isn't that difficult. You could outsmart three coaches, out hustle two more and outwork another five, which will leave you one coach with whom you may need to get lucky. In fact, to win your division you only have to outperform three other coaches.

**In many leagues, you only have to beat three other
coaches (teams) to make the playoffs.**

This is the typical coach you are up against: He believes he lives in that perfect fantasy football world. He attempts to draft the players he personally admires and then crosses his fingers that he will win his league championship and walk away with his ego intact, along with some cash. He takes his main tool, the NFL player rankings – obtained from magazines and Internet sites – plops it in front of the computer, does a wee bit of tweaking to show anyone who's interested in looking over his shoulder that he is an independent thinker, and hits the war room (the draft). At the end of the season, if he loses, he will blame some unfortunate stroke of luck and says to all who listen, "I'll be back next year." If this describes you, take heart! This book will show you how to dominate and win fantasy football championships.

Your opposition for the most part has no real strategy.
Outsmart, out hustle and outwork them and you will dominate.

OK, here's one last test. If you pass this, get ready to dominate.

My goal is to...
> Choice A - Have the best win-loss record in my league.
> Choice B - Win the championship game.

Choice A would be nice and could happen, but B is always your focus. Do not lose your way. I hope I'm making my point. It is easy to look at tomorrow or next week, but you want to keep your eye toward the end of the season now. If you are planning ahead and your opposition is only looking at tomorrow, dominating becomes much easier.

On one hand, you know you should be prudent. But on the other, you just want to enjoy yourself right now, be carefree, and do whatever. Let's face it – being the jester is more fun, but you won't win many championships playing the fool.

"Whatever, whatever, whatever".

3.4 - WHAT DOES IT TAKE TO WIN THE LEAGUE CHAMPIONSHIP?

A. Luck, History and Win-Loss Record

In this game, the fantasy football statistics are very important, but <u>not</u> the statistics you are currently looking at (projection numbers) in the magazines and web sites. Those statistics were born from your individual players and, yes, they will help you keep score during the season. But those numbers are secondary to the statistics related to putting together a championship team.

> **The current-year projection numbers are secondary numbers in setting up a championship team. Those numbers are available to everyone.**

Let's begin by breaking down some numbers. The numbers are the results you'll be measured by. Everything you do will end up as a number.

Your strategies should help increase your numbers or your odds in every facet of the game. Your opposition will have their strategies also, but I can guarantee they didn't do the numbers. It takes work! If you are willing to put in the work, that alone will be a huge advantage.

The first statistic you will need to grasp is the luck factor. For all intents and purposes, the fantasy football coaches and their teams start out equal. You have a 50 percent chance of winning and a 50 percent chance of losing. If you know luck is a big part of the fantasy football stage, you must work with and not against it. Accept it and work it into your team plan. You can greatly reduce the luck factor, but never eliminate it completely. Your goal is to bring the luck factor down to about 10 percent.

In most fantasy football leagues, luck is as high as 50 percent. You can reduce the luck factor to 10 percent, but you can never totally eliminate it.

If you would like to reduce your luck factor, you need to increase your knowledge of how the game should be played. This is called using strategies. True strategies, whether big or small, should always be focused on winning the championship game.

The opposite of strategies are the ideas, thoughts and good intentions a coach would like to see work, if we lived in a perfect world. Since we don't, a coach's best ideas will only take him so far.

The next statistics you need to know about are related to history. When an NFL coach wants to build a successful team, he looks to the past to analyze what other teams have done and tries to copy that same formula. You'll want to do the same. You'll want to look at the history of your league and see the patterns – not individual stats – which have been laid out time and time again and are just waiting for somebody like you to pay attention. History will reveal what your team will have to look like to be successful. History will repeat itself.

Many times, past performance is an indication of future results.

You'll need to look at last year's championships and search for anything that could help your team. While you're digging around last year's performances, it wouldn't hurt to analyze your team for what it did wrong. Always improve on your mistakes, as your mistakes are one thing that can be controlled. If you played in a league last year, your password is probably still good and you can look at the playoff rounds to see how each team won. Critique every angle – look for any holes in the rules you can take advantage of. I'm not advocating anything illegal, however. You need to play by the rules. But for every rule, you can take advantage of a strategy. For this year, keep a diary for each team you own and use that diary next year to improve your prospects. Look at the appendix at the end of this book for the set-up of your fantasy football diary.

Give yourself a history lesson. Analyze the league you played in last year. Keep a diary of your team(s) and use the analysis for next year's planning.

B. How can I reach the playoffs?

Of course, a major step in winning the championship is reaching the playoffs. It doesn't matter how you reach the playoffs as long as you get there, even if you have to bite, scratch and crawl. On the other hand, it does no good to have the best record in your league if you can't dominate the championship game. Your first mission is to achieve a good enough record to make the playoffs.

What record will you need to reach the playoffs? Let's examine that using last year's results. Look at the win records from below. (This is based on 21 leagues at CBS Sportsline).

Wins	# of Teams	Missed Playoffs	% Made Playoffs
14	0	0	—
13	0	0	—
12	6	0	100%
11	10	0	100%
10	18	1	94%
9	39	6	85%
8	41	23	44%

As you can see, nobody in my leagues won every game, although I'm sure in some league, somewhere, some team might have. Truthfully, it doesn't matter if you win all your games during the season, because when the playoffs begin, your record resets itself to 0-0. As the chart shows, winning nine or 10 games will put you in the playoffs the majority of the time. Winning just eight games, which is just one game above 500 in a 14 game fantasy football season, will get you to the playoffs almost 50 percent of the time. The goal here is to know what is needed to make the playoffs and make sure you get this far.

In the NFL, in any given week, any team can beat any other team. In fantasy football with head-to-head match ups, it's the same situation. In fact, finishing with the very best record and being the number one seed doesn't guarantee you the championship. A lower seeded team can easily win because the "any given Sunday" rule will hold true. You, the fantasy football coach, would like to break that rule, but winning the most games is not the way to do this. The way to dominate the championship game is to improve your team every week to the point where your team can't be touched.

In my leagues (not including my own teams), we had 12 teams with eight wins that made the playoffs. Two of those teams won the championships, which would suggest about a 16 percent winning factor. That doesn't show up very well in the final stat lines. I, personally, had three teams sneaking into the playoffs with eight wins. Championships were won in all three games (by Tweety, Gold Stars and Atomizers). Yes, I was fortunate to get into the playoffs, but when I got there, I had the teams to dominate the championship game.

You try to win every game and give it your best shot, but your focus must always be on the championship round. In knowing you can't or don't need to win every game, you may end up taking some losses during the season for the benefit of your goal. (Yes, you read that last statement correctly.)

You may have to give up some wins to make sure you dominate later. See section 8.6.

'Tis the season to give...wins.

C. How many points will I need to score?

In breaking down over 3,500 games, I have found the average score is 83.2 points. To win, of course, is to be above average. If you are above average, you'll probably win the majority of your games and have no problem reaching eight or more wins.

More important, however, is how many points the winning teams score. Now, you need to remember the "any given Sunday" rule. Even poor teams can score a "W" with a good score. Therefore, this is not the wins by the best teams for the season, but the winning scores for each week. The average is 94.8 for the first seven weeks and 96.1 for the last seven weeks. There wasn't much improvement there. That is great for you, as you can always take steps to improve your team while your opposition is standing around.

My teams' average score for the first seven weeks was 87.4, which was better than the average for all teams, but not good enough to beat the "winners" on any given Sunday. The last seven weeks, I improved my team to the tune of an average score of 104.4. Almost a 20 percent jump!

For the 2005 year, points scored during the playoffs averaged 92.5 points (not counting my teams). Did you notice how the good teams step up at the right time?

However, I was ready for them. My playoff teams averaged 109.7 points!

Do you see the correlation here? Improve your team as the year goes on, while the other coaches are just playing that particular week's game. Most coaches, by far, get serious about their teams too late in the season. If they start getting serious around Week 10, you have a 10-week (14 counting preseason) head start.

But, starting out after the draft, most teams will be pretty evenly matched in point scoring. After all, they all start from ground zero and the draft did what it was supposed to do in evenly distributing the players. No matter who you end up drafting, you want your team to get stronger as the season goes on and to show the greatest strength in the championship game. If this sounds like a fairy tale, let me tell you, it can be done.

Now, let's go back to that championship game and, as long as we're talking about fairy tales, let's assume every one of your starters came through and played very hard that day. That is the key. You want players who will show up and play hard for the championship game. You must use every resource to find those players.

Hard-Scoring Champion Team	
Position	**Points Scored**
QB	30
RB 1	20
RB 2	20
WR 1	15
WR 2	15
TE	15
K	10
D (defense)	20
Total	**145 points**

Boy, wouldn't that be wonderful?! You would probably win every game in every league. I can almost guarantee that you will not score 145 points. But you have just set your goal and you need to shoot toward that.

Let's look at the opposite end and say none of your players showed up to play that day. All of them scored about one-third of their best potential game. Total points would then be about 42. Most likely, you would lose 100 percent of the games. Somewhere in between the best and the worst is where you will probably end up.

In my research of the previous year, I found if I scored 100 points, I would win the majority of my league championships. Therefore, I set my goal to score 10 to 20 percent higher than the 100 points I needed to win. If I wanted to dominate, I needed players on my roster who could help me average 120 points per team.

In the first playoff week, my teams won 14 of 16 games for a dominating 87 percent win percentage and averaged 106.2 points per game.

In the championship round, my teams won 12 of the 14 games for, again, a dominating 85 percent win percentage and an average of 113.9 points a game.

The average winning difference was 34.2 points. It was like having 2 extra stud players on my team. It's definitely an advantage to play with ten men while my opposition plays with only eight.

Columbus scored 102 in 1492.

History repeats itself. Do the required research for your league.

It is possible to dominate as long as your strategies are all primed for the championship round. But the answers are rooted in what has happened in the past. History has already taught us what works...are we willing to learn?

D. What players do I need for the championship game?

We will answer this question in the next chapter, as the training camp is about to begin.

From the next chapter forward, you will find many strategies – some huge and some small – but all are important. There will be some strategies you won't have the opportunity to implement this year because it just did not fit a particular situation. You don't know when such a situation will come up, but, as the coach, you need to be ready.

The next chapter, "Training Camp," will start to lay out the strategies you need in order to dominate. This will be the most important chapter for you to understand, as your competition regards this very lightly. In fact, 99 percent of fantasy football players have no idea this step exists. Training Camp will set the foundation for your championship run.

WARNING! All of the information is this book is based on a standard league roster and performance scoring. If you play in a non-standard league, it is your responsibility to understand how any or all of the strategies can impact your team.

CHAPTER 4

WELCOME TO TRAINING CAMP:
Gear Up for a Dominating Season

WHAT YOU WILL LEARN:

1. How to build your team roster to dominate
2. How to set up a customized color-coded pre-draft cheatsheet
3. The benefits of tiering
4. How to maximize your 'bility
5. The most important position in your draft
6. How to pick a league
7. Why you need assistant coaches

Overview

This is the most important chapter in the book. In it, you will learn how to select the best players for your team, not only for the draft (also known as the "war room") but for the entire season. Just like a head coach in the NFL, you will learn to analyze your team roster from many perspectives, and many of these – such as bye weeks, game day weather and home-field advantage – have little to do with the players as individuals. But they are key to your overall roster strategy.

The exciting part? Most of your opposition won't think this way. They will give very little regard to a strategic roster designed to win the championship game. At the time of the draft, they will have no clue that their teams are already several steps behind yours in the race for the big game. As far as they are concerned, this was just another draft. This will be clear by the end of Chapter 5.

Training camp is needed to make sure your roster strategies and your draft strategies work hand-in-hand for the team effort.

In the NFL, training camp is the foundation for a successful season. The head coaches use this time to accomplish many functions. The coaches evaluate their players, not only to see who is best at each position, but to determine who fits into their overall team concept. This concept drives their overall philosophy of what the team can handle in the beginning, and ensures the proper steps to grow as the season progresses. If a coach does not utilize his training camp to the greatest benefit, it will indeed be a long, arduous season. Every coach is also aware he cannot accomplish what needs to be done alone and needs his assistant coaches. He must fully utilize his $100 million NFL player-cap payroll.

The fantasy football coach should also conduct his or her own training camp. Ours is a bit different in that our evaluation of the players is for the upcoming draft. However, there are many similarities. We must find the players who fit our "team concept," lay out our philosophy for the entire season, know we will need to grow as the season progresses, have some gimmick plays available and hire some assistant coaches. The training camp is our foundation for a successful season. It will set your war room up correctly and also set the tone throughout the season. Most of your opposition does not understand the importance of this step.

Luckily for us, it does not cost $100 million for player salaries, only an entry fee and about $100 bucks for some assistant coaches and our time. (See section 9.1 for more about the assistant coaches.)

The War Room Chapter will be more in-depth and focus only on the draft. You, however, need to focus on how you choose *to do* the draft.

On the following lines, please write down the players you covet. (These are the studs you want based entirely on emotion.)

_____   _____

_____   _____

When you complete this chapter, take a look back and see how many of these players you still want on your team.

4.1 - PREPARING YOUR PERSONALIZED CHEATSHEET

To truly dominate your fantasy football league, you must start with your preferred player list. These are the players you need on your team, the ones who will perform consistently, who will play hard and score points when you need them the most – in the championship game. These players are not necessarily the ones that you want (like above), and certainly not the players that most of your opposition will covet.

Your preferred player list will be generated from your own personalized colored-coded cheatsheet. To prepare, you need three items: 1) the latest ranking sheet for all positions, taken from either the Internet or a fantasy football magazine, 2) the NFL schedule for the coming season and 3) a computer with a spreadsheet software program. Don't try to do this by hand, as you will end up with something that looks like a Picasso instead of a handy chart to guide you through the complex draft process.

Step One

Open your spreadsheet software program and create a separate spreadsheet for each team position.

Step Two

Create four columns in each spreadsheet – one column for the player's first name (or initial if you prefer), one column for the player's last name, one column for the player's bye week and the last column for the player's projected points. (You will use the projected points only as a quick reference when the draft clock is down to five seconds.)

Your columns will look like this:

FIRST (INIT.)	LAST NAME	BYE WEEK	PROJ. PTS.
C.	Dillon	10	225
T.	Barber	5	195

Step Three

Determine the number of players to rank on each spreadsheet by looking at how many are expected to be drafted. At CBS Sportsline, they have a pretty regimented draft. You'll see 24 QB, 45 RB, 40 WR, 24 TE, 12 K and 24 defenses picked. Therefore, don't put every player in the NFL on the sheet, instead put about 10 percent more than what will actually be drafted. When you get that deep, you'll find players' names you have never heard of and most likely do not need on your team; therefore, going any further is a waste of time. You may need others during the season, but we are only concerned about preparing for the draft at this point.

Step Four

Type the ranking for each position in the exact order projected by your source. This will take some work but, believe me, it will be worth it.

Note: Be certain the projected points reflect your fantasy football league's scoring system (or close to it), otherwise the projected points are not only of no value, but can be detrimental to quick decision-making. See section 2.3 for more information about selecting a fantasy football league.

Take your time and input everything before you continue reading.

Step Five

Now that you have the experts' rating of the players for each position, you need to tweak it for your own personal ranking. This has nothing to do with the draft order, only the order in which **you** believe the players should be projected. If you need a guide, use the list below (and/or your own gut instincts) to evaluate each of the players on whether or not you feel they will over-perform or under-perform and move them up or down on your spreadsheet accordingly.

Note: Remember to cut and paste all four columns each time and **do not change the projected points scored**.

Possible reasons players may under-perform:
1. He has off-field problems
2. His attitude is negative
3. His body is prone to injury
4. His team is rebuilding
5. He is working with a rookie quarterback
6. His age is catching up with him
7. His team can't penetrate the red zone
8. He is performing poorly in training camp
9. Other(s) _____

Possible reasons players over-perform:
1. He is playing an increased role in his team's offense
2. He is playing on a team with a softer schedule
3. He has a new offensive coordinator
4. He is playing with a new offense more suited to his talents
5. He finished strong last year
6. His team has additional offensive weapons

7. He has less competition at his specific position
8. He is in the last year of his contract
9. His stats have improved annually
10. He is having a great camp
11. Other(s) _____

This will not be the last time you tweak your spreadsheets before the draft. When you hear news – good or bad – you may want to move the players around. But let's discuss the rankings that you just tweaked.

While the experts' picks and projections are good tools, every fantasy football player in the land is armed with them. Further, they are generally misused. Many coaches mistakenly take them as an accurate guide because they rarely go back after the season is over and examine the projected stats against the actual stats.

> **We would all love to be able to predict with uncanny accuracy the projected points and subsequent rankings for the year end, but since that is impossible, you need to be satisfied searching out your overall strategies.**

However, you don't have to look at actual stats year by year as long as you know the patterns. The history of the past for the most part will repeat itself in the future. Let history guide you. For example, look at the current rankings in your spreadsheet and see whose names are in the top 10 for each position. How confident are you that the top 10 in the preseason will end up (in some order) the same top 10 at the end of the year?

All 10? 9? 8?

Come on, this is the cream of the crop for each position! How many?

I went back the last five years for each position to see how many players repeated the following year. See section **10.3** for the Annual Top Ten Repeaters chart.

> **The rankings are more art than exact science. Treat them accordingly. Use history as your guide.**

Most seasons, you'll be lucky if there are five of the top 10 players left at the end of the season. There are many reasons for a player not to repeat the following year. Injuries are the leading cause. I would like to make two points. 1). All the so-called experts are right only 50 percent of the time; therefore, you need not rely on these rankings as an exact projection. 2). You will also make the right choice only 50 percent of the time. Don't be upset with yourself. There are just too many variables.

Remember, all the other coaches are in the same boat. In fact, most will only take the expert's cheatsheets and make a few notes. By typing this customized list into your computer and tweaking your players, you have now done more work than 80 percent of the players out there today. However, you have not really helped yourself out – yet. But, the hardest part is behind you.

Step Six
You're now going to use the spreadsheets you created as a customized cheatsheet to identify your preferred players. This is one of the smartest steps toward domination because it helps you realize your league's scoring potential before you begin. The colors are important – they indicate your preferred players. The preferred players will be on the list for many different reasons, and some will be *more* preferred than others. To do the coding, you can choose any color you like, as long as you have four

different colors. You'll be coloring the boxes (fill in) and the fonts to help differentiate your preferred players. Only colored-coded names should make your preferred players list. However, that doesn't mean you would skip over a stud to get a lesser player. All things must come in their own time during the draft.

The customized colored cheatsheet is one of the smartest steps toward domination. You must know your league's scoring tendencies before you begin. See section 2.3 for more information on selecting a league.

We need to find the players that have the Fantasy Football Real Value (FFRV) to your team. This is subjective to each coach for his own reasons. It will tell you how to build your team. When you are done, you will look at two evenly rated players (via the experts' projections) and easily choose the one that has the highest FFRV for your team. This is not unlike the NFL, where they may have two equal RBs (as far as speed goes) but one RB will stand out because he fits with the type of blocking his team has implemented. It is a "no-brainer" for the NFL coach and, now that you will have your cheatsheet, it will be a no brainer for you.

Find the potential from your player's perspective.

As in the NFL, fantasy football is a team sport. Repeat after me, "team sport." We all want that number one super stud on our team, but this super stud is only a part of your championship run. **Every one of your starters must have the potential to score big in the championship game.**

Let's breakdown that sentence. "Every one of your starters" means all eight positions. No weak spots. After the draft, you will have some weak spots, as every coach will (I call these weak spots warts), but it's your job during the season to clean up your warts. You can't hope to have your best team in Week 1. You must always look to improve and that is the secret – **you need to choose which position you will start weak**. "Must have the potential" means you pick players for your team based on the **likelihood of them shining in the championship game**. For instance, I don't want to see my RB2 going up against the 2005 Chicago Bears defense in Chicago with the wind chill hovering at zero degrees. "To score big" means **more points for your team** toward that fairytale ending of 145 points (see section 3.4).

Before the draft, choose which roster spot you want to start in the weakest position. Act, don't react.

Let's make sure you get the point. The opposite of a team sport is to have one super stud surrounded by role players. Can that stud carry your team all year long on his back and, even more important, in the championship game? Let's look at the names of the players usually drafted in the first five picks in 2005 (based on my 21 leagues) to find out.

Peyton Manning
LaDainian Tomlinson
Shaun Alexander
Priest Holmes
Edgerrin James

If we look at the championship fantasy football Week 16, we'll see which players were instrumental in helping their coach win the championship.

Peyton Manning	0%
LaDainian Tomlinson	0%
Shaun Alexander	24%
Priest Holmes	0%
Edgerrin James	0%

As you can see, the super stud didn't have a huge impact in championship rounds (every year could be different). Remember, always keep your team concept in mind. Yes, you will draft for the studs, but respect that they are only one player of your team. This coming year, there will be new top-five players and possibly the next year even five different players.

There is no "I" in team. Individuals can win games but a team can consistently dominate games.

You'll be tempted to say this year is different and that, my friend, will be a huge error. Have there ever been fantasy football players who literally carried their team on their backs from the first game all the way to winning the championship? Absolutely, it happens about once every decade. Once in 10 years is not the type of odds you want to put on your side.

As you prepare for the draft, you must use the same common sense the NFL does in their college drafts. Take players that fill up the weak spots for your team or are the best athletes available. Do not let the strategies override your common sense.

Let your disciplined strategies and your common sense intelligence work hand-in-hand.

Step Six A: Find the "Easy-Match" Players

You have a 50/50 chance of a particular player meeting the projections or flopping. What is a coach to do? Easy, use the matchup strategy.

Since you can't know with any certainty which player is best to draft, you must look ahead and focus on what you *do* know. In this case, you want to draft the players who will show up to play for you in the championship game. This is not as hard as it sounds. For example: Would you rather have Larry Johnson playing at home running against a weak '49er defense or Shaun Alexander playing on the road against the tough Steelers? Pretty easy choice, wasn't it? If your turn in the draft comes and both players are available for you, it is a slam-dunk.

So start by looking at the strength of the *teams* for that particular week.

Using the match-up strategy during the draft is a huge key to out-playing your opposition in the championship game.

Find your championship week from your league. If you want, you can also include the playoff week, but focus on the championship week. In CBS Sportsline, it will be Week 16. Highlight Weeks 15 (the first playoff round) and 16 on the NFL schedule. Based on your current knowledge of these teams' performance, circle the teams that look to be the weakest. Yes, you are guessing, but you are using your past experience, just as the so-called experts do. Those weak team's **opponent's players** are the ones you want to put on your team because they have greater likelihood of scoring huge fantasy points for your team. This is called "playing match up." Roughly 50 percent of your championship-week starters should come from this strategy. Every fantasy football player understands how match ups work, but you are almost the **only one** who will look at match ups today with the end of the season in mind.

Get the first name (or initial, if that is what you used) of any player playing against a weak team for Week 16 and fill that square with yellow. Great players, good players, poor players, it does not matter – highlight them all with yellow. These are the players who will tend to have an easy game precisely when you need them to. They will make your team hot when it needs to be hot.

Any yellow-highlighted player who also plays against a weak team for your playoffs (Week 15) will get their first name in red font. It might give you an extra incentive if a certain player has both a yellow highlight and a red font. I'm not saying these players will actually play for you at the end of the season, although the odds are they will. The odds are also in your favor that they will potentially score a high number of points. As the season wears on, you will want to keep on the lookout for these players. They may be available at some point on the waiver wire or for trading.

We have more to do on this strategy later, but you have just taken the first step.

Step Six B: The Weather Man

Right now you're reading this book during the preseason and the weather across the United States is, for the most part, very nice. During Week 16, the championship round, there will be many games played in poor weather. You would prefer your players to not have to deal with the weather. It has the possibility to limit their potential. You may want to put an asterisk (*) next to any player's first name that has been yellow highlighted who may possibly be playing the championship round in the winter cold. You still want this player, but maybe you won't be quite as sold on him if there is a comparable player available. You would prefer players on teams who play in domes and or with southern exposure.

In 2005, there were actually no games in Week 16 that were adversely hampered by the weather. Of course, you can't know that going into the following year. Hedge your odds if you can.

The weather has the ability to influence your key games at the end of the season.

As a side note, you would love it if your strong defense was playing a weak team at home in a snowstorm! You don't want to forget those defenses. They are part of your team.

Step Six C: The Home Field Advantage

Simply put, home is where the heart is. Players who are on their home field usually perform better; therefore, for any player playing at home in Week 16, put an "**H**" next to any yellow highlighted player's bye week. If he is scheduled at home, it might further narrow down your choices. Is there any team playing both Weeks 15 and 16 at home? The home field advantage will come into play again when working with the bye weeks in the next section.

Home Sweet Home

Your cheatsheet should now have yellow highlights with red fonts, asterisks (*) and "H"s, all over the pages, from the top studs to the lowly role player. These are your "easy-match" players. The easy-match players have the highest **potential** to score points for your team.

> **Statistically, ninety-nine percent of football players play better games at home. Find players that play at home during the championship game.**

Step Six D: Handling the Bye Week

Most fantasy football players hate the bye weeks, but they truly can be used to your advantage. In fact, the bye week is a definite "two-fer" situation, if handled correctly. In the NFL, as mentioned above, the team playing at home has a built-in bias. Their fans are like an extra player or an extra charge to the team, whatever you want to call it, but the home field advantage is real. When you play against a team that has one or more of their starters sitting on the bench, while you have all your starter's strength, you truly have the "home field advantage". If you play this home field advantage to the max each bye week, you have gained a full game on your opposition over the season.

How does this work?

You'll want to find a combination of strong NFL teams (teams that score many points will probably score many fantasy points) that also have their bye weeks toward the end of the bye-week season. We're hoping for Weeks 8, 9 and 10. Highlight (fill in) with green the **last names** of players who are on strong teams (the opposition does not matter) and are on a bye on one of those three weeks.

> **NEWS FLASH:** *In 2006 the Week 10 bye was eliminated and those teams were squeezed into Week 6 & 7. This makes those weekends potentially precarious and possibly advantageous for fantasy football players who are aware. Also, starting Week 12, the league has many more Thursday night games. Whether this has a positive or negative impact on your strategies is up to you.*

Now let's get out there and bye, bye, bye.

At this point, if you have any multicolored highlighted player, you should strongly consider putting him on your team. Players highlighted in green are part of your preferred players list.

> **There are many different advantages to be had during the bye week. Embrace them.**

Why are players with late bye weeks advantageous?

More time to fill your empty roster spots. As the NFL season progresses, there will be more choices of players popping out of the woodwork each week that no one has on their roster. *That's a guarantee.* It happens year in and year out. You'll use the waiver wire, as will your opposition, to pick up as many of these future gems as possible. Having your team filled up with late byes will give you that much more time to cover your empty roster spots. There will be fewer choices in the early season and the competition will be strong. After Week 8, some losing fantasy football teams will be less interested overall and there will be fewer teams vying for the player pool. As a coach, I would much rather have to fill my roster spots in Week 9 than in Week 3.

> **Having an "extra" player because this week's opponent is affected negatively by a bye week is like having the home field advantage. Home teams usually win!**

In the early part of the season, you will always be starting your strongest team. Your opposition may have weak spots because of the early bye weeks on their team. Won't it be fun to play them when their stud is on a bye? That is like having home field advantage!

More time to recover from injuries. Injuries can happen anytime, but they happen more frequently as the season wears on. NFL football players are warriors but injuries, especially nagging ones, will crop up. Having your players on a bye week in Week 9 may be just what the doctor ordered to give them some much-needed rest so they can gear up for the remaining part of the season.

Players with late byes are a huge advantage over the earlier byes, if said players will fit your overall strategies.

Willie Roaf, one of the top linemen in the NFL, needed rest for his hamstring (in 2005) and it affected the whole team's production. A bye week in the NFL is more valuable in the latter part of the season. It should be for your fantasy football team also.

More time to trade up. You can possibly trade for a player midseason that has already been on an early bye for your player who has a late bye. Your team essentially could avoid a bye for that position. Wouldn't that be sweet?!

Take advantage of "bunching." Find the teams that are off in the same week. There are four NFL teams off per week in Weeks 3 through 9 (12 percent of the teams). In 2006, Weeks 6 & 7 will have six teams off (almost 20 percent). Ouch. If you can find a late bye week in which three of the four teams are powerhouses and they **also** have your highlighted players, then you have hit a gold mine.

Look at putting at least your first two picks and more, if possible, off on the same week. There have been many articles written by fantasy football experts about having "all" (for the sake of the argument) of your players off on the same week or spreading the bye weeks of your players through-out the season. You must choose a direction yourself, but the math has proven that having your strongest team playing each week, except for that one bye week, is the way to go. However (and this is the kicker, pardon the pun), you still need not worry for, as long as you choose the late bye weeks, you will have plenty of time to pick up strong replacements. This strategy essentially gives you a one-game advantage over your opposition.

Dominate Fantasy Football

Need I go on? Do not fear the bye week syndrome but embrace it.

If you handle the NFL bye week situation correctly, you will find several "home" games you are playing and can pick up an additional game in your league by becoming strong on your late week "bunching" strategy.

Step Six E: Find the "Even-Keel" Players

You want to highlight the players you believe will consistently – and that is the key word – *consistently* score points. If you had two wide receivers that both scored 175 fantasy football points by year's end, you would think they would be equal for your team. They are not. You would much rather have the wide receiver who will score an average of 11 points per week than the wide receiver who scores 33 points one week and zero for the next two weeks. These players are your true studs. So choose the players you believe will score consistently and use the font color blue on the projected number (do not change the number).

If there is any doubt about a player's ability to score consistently, then walk away. There are plenty of players from which to choose, let the other coaches scoop him up.

Consistency is important. If you feel your running back or wide receiver has the *potential* to score at least one touchdown each week and also has the *potential* to put up a solid (but not spectacular) 80 yards, then that is the consistency you want for your team. You'll find this mostly in your top 10 for each position. On the other hand, if you spot a good RB and the NFL team drafts a rookie, creating a RBBC-type situation, stay away from that player, as his consistency rating just took a hit. Let your opposition take the risk.

Step Six F: Tracking Down Gold Star Candidates

Your next assignment is to find one or more Gold Star candidates. These will probably come from your top elite running backs. Find the teams that have the most powerful offensive lines. We're talking an offensive line that will blow holes big enough to drive a Mack truck through. (Hint: look at your offensive linemen who went to the Pro Bowl last year.) Whoever this running back is, you'll take him. You realize if this running back goes down, his backup will probably run about as well. That means you have locked in one RB position, even if an injury were to happen. When you look at your running back studs, consider the system surrounding him. You want a stud that will get the goal line carries. No doubt every other coach also covets these Gold Star candidates, but you are looking for the ones with the multiple colors on their names for your overall team concept.

In 2005, the running backs who fit these criteria were Shaun Alexander, Priest Holmes, and E. James with Seattle, Kansas City and Indianapolis, respectively.

Shhhh, I'm hunting Running Back.

For the year you are drafting in, you'll need to find those special offensive lines and fill the bye week with the color red. These will be the Gold Star studs.

Have you chosen enough players yet? I'm sure you've chosen more than 14, which is the maximum allowed on your roster. But, since you don't know which ones will be available by the time your draft pick snakes around, you want to have the flexibility to choose the players with a highest potential for your team.

Step Seven: Spot Your "Must Have" Players
By now you should have on each spreadsheet:
  "Easy-Match" Players
- Yellow fill-in on first name —easy players with the potential for high scoring championship points
- Red font on first name – players playing a weak opponent in the playoff

Asterisk (*) Next to the First Name – players possibly playing in the cold weather, pare him down a bit

"H" next to the player's bye week – players with a home-field advantage for championship

Green fill-in on the last name – strong players or teams during late bye weeks

Blue font on the projected stats – consistent weekly scorers = solid and dependable

Red fill-in for the bye week – the Gold Star elite RBs = studs

See any candidates that have all three fill in colors? Those are your "must have" players. Find a way to put them on your team. The more colors a player collects on your ranking sheets, the more he becomes preferred to you. His FFRV (Fantasy Football Real Value) is high to your team. That same player may not be high to your opposition, which is great for you. In fact, your opposition only sees "similar" players.

As you put your FFRV on players, keep in mind to resist getting carried away and drafting them too early.

Stats are secondary to your team concept and the FFRV (Fantasy Football Real Value) indicates which players you want on your team.

Step Eight: Tiering – Group Your Players

Tiering is much like the VBD (which we'll discuss in the War Room Chapter). Where the VBD will rate players on an individual basis, tiering will put players together as a group. Most often, the players are grouped using the projected points on your ranking sheet. If you have seven running backs that are projected to score within 24 points of each other, you could put them in a tier together. One running back in that group is probably as good as any of the other running backs. If they would finish the season exactly as the projected points state, with the poorest running back scoring 24 points less than the best running back, divide that by 15 (16 fantasy football weeks - one bye week) and note that you are talking less than two points per game. Not a big enough margin to lose sleep over. Of course, when the season ends, the projected points will not be correct but, for today, that is the math you have to use. Therefore, any running backs in that particular tier are the same to you.

Warning! Since you have tweaked your cheatsheet and left the projections numbers intact, you must do your own boxes based on the way you see the players performing and for the moment ignore the experts' projections. Your cheatsheet will not be presented in a neat package such as the example on the next page.

Here's a tiering example:

RB1 projected points of 226
RB2 projected points of 218
RB3 projected points of 205 *
RB4 projected points of 197
RB5 projected points of 192

RB6 projected points of 179
RB7 projected points of 174
RB8 projected points of 171
RB9 projected points of 165
RB10 projected points of 165
RB11 projected points of 159*
RB12 projected points of 154

* a player from your "preferred player list"

As you can see, the RB1 through RB5 would be your first tier of running backs. The RB6 through RB12 would be your second tier of running backs. The number of tiers is completely up to you, but create them for each position. If the above were your draft and you are to have the fourth pick and your RB3 was already gone, you wouldn't drop down to RB11. You would be giving up too many points. You would instead draft RB4 or RB5. You want to follow your strategy, but you still have to use your common sense. Since there are 11 other coaches, I can guarantee you won't get every player you desire, but as long as you are flexible, you will put together a solid team.

Tiering will allow you to look at the players in each position as a group.

Here is the real benefit of tiering. When your draft choice comes and there are six out of seven running backs left in that particular tier, you will realize, in looking ahead, that at your next draft pick, there will still be some of those running backs left from that tier. So, you then jump to a different position (i.e., the wide receivers), which only has one player left in its tier. Scoop up the WR and wait for the RB on your next turn. Now you are drafting smart.

As part of the evolution of fantasy football, all the serious fantasy football players tier their players before draft day. With the tweaking you did earlier, you already put your players in a tier. You just didn't know it yet. You'll now want to go back to your customized cheatsheet and draw boxes around the group of players you feel are close to each other in projected points. You must ignore all the coloring you did in the previous steps and just focus on drawing boxes.

Start with one position, such as the running backs. Your first box is your elite running backs. It does not matter if the box contains two or 12 players, that is your choice. You are designating that all running backs grouped within that particular box are the same, looking only at projected points, from your view, not the FF experts. Now after you do a box for the elite, draw a box for the solid RBs, next make a box for the "average" RBs, then the marginal or poor RBs. There should be four boxes in all.

Do the same for each position. As you form the boxes, there are some things that will stick out. The drop off point from the elite RB to the solid RB is not really great, but from the elite WRs to the next box of WR is large. In fact, it really goes from elite to average and then the point drop off is pretty steep. (We will discuss this further in the next chapter.) Did you notice how many solid QBs there are?

Now that you have your boxes drawn around the players, you can "look" at your colored-coded players' names. Do you have several colored-coded players in each tier? When you draft in a certain tier, try to get the player you have marked as preferred. But do not drop a tier until the one above it is all drafted out. When should you go from the RB tier box to the WR tier box? That will be covered in the next chapter in section 5.13.

> **Keep all players on the customized spreadsheets, not just the ones you have highlighted. You'll still need to look at the big picture at all times.**

You can learn more about tiering at FantasyFootballChamps.com. In fact, they have done all the work for you if you want to use their expertise and not your own.

As you have been customizing your cheatsheet, I hope you have only "tweaked" and did not change the overall rankings to a large degree. You want all the players to be located approximately where the majority of the people believe they should be ranked. This ranking sheet is not just for your benefit, but also for you to see what your opposition is contemplating. You'll consider, in order to save time, only listing the players you want on the sheet. That won't give you a complete picture. Give yourself the freedom to tweak the sheet, use spaces in between to separate your tiering, and color your "preferred choices."

You'll have more than one choice in each tier you draft from. If you don't, you can now see where your draft may be weak and need to mark another pick or two via your sleeper list, heart or crystal ball.

Your customized worksheet is now better than 80 percent of the other fantasy football players' tools and will be a solid help for your strategies. However, you need to leave your cheatsheet alone for now and move on to what your roster should look like. You will open your cheatsheet up again in the next chapter to test it out.

> **Mark your ranking sheet and identify the "preferred" players to play as a team. Grab as many of these as reasonably possible during the draft and throughout the NFL season. You would be honored if they would play for your team.**

4.2 - GET THE 'BILITY

The #1 rule in fantasy football is to have the 'bility. You must be able to show your "flexibility" and your "adjustability" throughout the season. Your goal is to look at your opposition and be 100-200 percent more flexible and adjustable than they are. **WOW!** While your opposition may have two bench players available for an interchange, you will have four to six interchangeable bench players. You need to make them think you have eight arms and are everywhere at the same time. Places they are thinking about going, you have already been there and have implemented into your team.

Okay, which one of you pinched me?

'Bility relates to your entire roster of players on your fantasy football team. On your team, you'll have eight starters and six bench players. This is what many of your opposition will have on their 14-player roster:

3 QB	3 RB	4 WR	1 TE	1 K	2 DEF
2 QB	3 RB	3 WR	2 TE	2 K	2 DEF
2 QB	3 RB	3 WR	2 TE	2 K	2 DEF
4 QB	3 RB	3 WR	1 TE	1 K	2 DEF

These are typical rosters, but its makeup is determined by each individual coach and may change throughout the year. Do you see any problems? Of course not, this was probably just like the teams you have had in the past. You like your team and you have rationalized that every player on your roster is important to your needs. If every player is important, let me ask you a question. How many of your players starting the NFL season in Week 1 will be on your team in Week 14 (the end of the fantasy football regular season)?

Write down your guess_____

Don't read on until you filled in the box above. It's important that you understand this point not only for this chapter but also for the Waiver Warrior Chapter.

I would suggest that you have never gone back in your previous years of playing fantasy football and looked at this stat for your team, but it is very important to know. What you drafted or what you started with in the first week will never be the team you end up with. If it is, I guarantee you will finish last in your division. You must always strive to improve your team and the 'bility will empower you to do this. The bottom line is the 'bility will allow you more of what every fantasy football player desires. You will increase your possibilities for playing match ups, two-fers, holding future gems and others. The list is endless and depends on what your team needs are.

The #1 rule is to create space on your bench by using your 'bility to outmaneuver your entire league. Maximizing this will increase your overall potential by 10 to 15 percent in points scored.

History tells us (yep, another history lesson) the average team will have about 50 percent of the roster intact at the end of the fantasy football season and be ready for the playoffs (see section 10.4.). Therefore, if your guess was 6, 7 or 8, I will give you a gold star for the day. The championship teams all have this high roster turnover as a solid trait.

Now that you realize from day one you will need turnover to grow and improve as the season goes on, you need to give yourself the maximum 'bility available.

This is the roster you should be striving for on NFL Week 1:

| 3 QB | 5 RB | 3 WR | 1 TE | 1 K | 1 DEF |

OR

| 2 QB | 7 RB | 2 WR | 1 TE | 1 K | 1 DEF |

Do you see the difference? To receive something, you have to give up something. You will have to live (for most of the season) with one tight end, one kicker, and one defense.

The running back position is the most crucial position during the season. You must be able to pick up running backs at every available opportunity and there will be many opportunities during the season. Your opposition will also love to pickup the running backs, but their roster will limit them.

> **Prepare for an annual 50 percent turnover rate and plan accordingly. You actually need that turnover to properly improve your team over the season. Champions follow this trait wholeheartedly.**

Every one of your teams (if you have multiple teams) will have different needs, depending on many variables, but the importance of having 'bility over your opposition will remain consistent. You have six bench players and you need to be smart about using them.

If you apply this book's lessons, you'll be the strongest over the entire season at the running back position, although not in the beginning. The running back position will open up many opportunities for you to dominate. Having many running backs is not one-dimensional. Warning: this is your roster speaking, not your draft. I am not saying draft all your RBs early on! Quite the contrary, if you do this, you will surely flounder.

> **Running backs are golden. You cannot have too many. But you can't start out strong with RBs or you will lose over the season.**

Your goal is to have more running backs over the NFL season than anyone else in your league. You have more possibilities for playing match ups, trading, and watching which running backs develop as the season progresses.

Injuries are part of the NFL season, so more running backs will be available as the year wears on – guaranteed. Toward the end of the season, they will be falling from the trees.

Let us examine this a bit deeper. Think "match ups" (at any position). Would you rather play Brett Favre against the Chicago defense or Brett Favre against the 49ers defense? Would you rather run Rudi Johnson on the road in beautiful weather against the Oakland Raiders or run Willis McGahee at home in a blizzard against Pittsburgh Steelers? During the season, many of your choices will be for the match ups, if you have any choices at all. Your job is to stockpile your future choices.

Let's go back to the positions on your roster, of which you only have one (at least most of the time):

Can kickers play match up? To a point, possibly, but not really. They will be pretty consistent for their team.

Can the tight ends match up? For the most part, no way. The average tight end will give you four points per week. If you're trying to decide between two points and six points, then you are not serious about dominating fantasy football.

Bring it on.

Can the defense match up? Yes, they possibly could, but if you pick a top-notch defense, you'll treat them like your stud running backs and play them regardless of any match up. The bottom line is, if you can't play match up with a certain position, you only need one player at that position.

What about injuries? That is one of the trade-offs you must take into consideration but, really, how many kickers get injured in a year? If your TE is injured, his replacement is going to a big four-pointer anyway. What about the bye weeks? Good question, and the answer will surprise you, but will come later.

Therefore, the match ups you wish to take advantage of are, for the most part, with the QBs, RBs and the WRs. Which of those positions has the most injuries during the season? The RBs, of course. If you have fewer opportunities to pick up good QBs and WRs, don't put yourself in that position in the first place. Make sure your WRs and QBs are as strong as possible from the beginning.

In conclusion, you need to strengthen your match up possibilities. The more bench roster spots you created through your 'bility, the more they will help you fill holes and particular needs for your team throughout the season. Now you can make adjustments easily. This 'bility will take you to the head of the class in the Waiver Wire Warrior Chapter. I guarantee your opposition will be scratching their heads and wondering how one team can be everywhere at once. Tell them you just have the 'bility and smile broadly.

4.3 - WHAT OTHER PLAYERS SHOULD YOU CONSIDER?

Sleepers

The "sleeper" players are those that no one else is expecting to perform well, but do. Look at last year's players who were injured for much of the season as they make excellent sleeper candidates. You should also check out the NFL schedule to see which teams will have an easier schedule over the entire season as compared to the previous year. Players on those teams might be able to pad their stats. There is nothing more exciting in a season than picking a sleeper that works out for your team.

Grabbing a sleeper at any point in the draft gives your team some upside potential for little risk.

While trolling for sleepers, you should also look at the RBs. Always strongly consider a running back's age. The older the running back, the more opportunities for injury. (Especially the nagging kind.) Their bodies take longer to heal as compared to a 24 year-old. If a running back is above age 30, I will look strongly at their backup for my sleeper. You can expect your average running back to miss two to three games a year. Odds are greater that the older running back will miss more than that.

Backups to an older running back should not be drafted but watch them carefully during the season. Be ready to pounce when your assistant coaches say so.

Quarterbacks

These players are pivotal to your roster, but, just as I demonstrated during our cheatsheet exercise, there are many factors to consider when choosing one. What about a quarterback who will not necessarily win games in the NFL but, because their team plays from behind much of the time, be forced to throw? The more a quarterback throws, the more opportunities for yards and touchdowns. A quarterback on a poor NFL team could be a strong quarterback for your fantasy football team.

If you have a very strong NFL passing team, you should consider pairing up the quarterback and wide receiver for your fantasy football team.

Try to score one quarterback from a poor NFL team with
a very low draft pick or even on the waiver wire. The risk is low
(and you have the potential to play match ups) but the
rewards could be great.

4.4 - WHAT PLAYERS SHOULD YOU NOT CONSIDER?

When creating our list of favored players, switch tactics and weed out the players you want to *avoid*. These are the players you do *not* want playing on our team. Some are stronger than others, but you want them to play on your opposition's team.

Take the opposite tact of what you previously did and make sure you do not get players that have tough assignments during the championship week. The exception would be your super studs. Again, I do not *prefer* my #1 RB stud to have his hardest game of the year in the championship week. In fact, you can guarantee this won't happen by not drafting that particular player.

For your fantasy football championship week on the NFL schedule, you will need to look at the match ups. Play the good match
ups, and stay away from the bad.

Rookies!

Yes, there will be a rookie every year that will tear up the NFL, but trying to pick which rookie is worse than the 50 percent rule. Most rookies hit a wall during the season because their bodies and minds are not accustomed to a full 17-game NFL season. Their stats will be consistently lower as the season wears on, especially when you need them the most for the championship game. There are also those rookies who get tied up in the contract negotiations, sit out part of pre-season, and never do catch up as they end up riding the pine most of the year. Let your opposition go gaga over the latest rookie hype.

Players must prove themselves in the NFL and, until they do, they cannot play for your team. No rookies.

Problem players, whiners and overall crybabies.

These players have no place on your team no matter how attractive they look. These players may have all the tools in the world, but they seem to consistently find a way to sabotage themselves. Don't let them set foot on your team. Randy Moss and Terrell Owens come to mind (sorry boys). Don't put them on your team at any price. If they come back to haunt you, realize you were just playing the odds. The odds favor you.

Gimme the ball. Gimme the ball.

Players on teams going through changes.

Some changes can be good and will work out for the benefit of everybody; however, most changes take time and you'll see a drop in the stats. The reason is because somebody has to bend to someone else's new philosophy and buy into his program. It takes time to adjust. If you see a new coach, temper your expectations for those players. If a great defense from the previous year loses their defensive coach, modify that defense's stats downward. When an NFL player switches teams, you'll usually find his stats won't increase. I'm not advocating staying away like the plague, but just temper down.

On the other hand, the longer a player is a part of a particular team, familiarity is bred and can lead to increased production.

Personnel changes usually take the greater part of the season to have a positive impact. At around Week 10, look at all the teams, bad or good, to see if they are playing stronger in any phase then they did in the beginning of the year. If it's not related to an easier schedule, it could be because they are playing better as a team. Look at players from those teams, since they might be getting stronger as the year goes on. They might become a good pick up or trade down the road.

During the preseason, there is much hype. Hype is always unsubstantiated. If the media does the hyping, you know it's just to sell their own product. If the player himself is doing the hyping, run away as fast as you can. However, if the coach is the one dishing out the hype on one of his players, I would lean in and listen. The coach has the ability in his play calling to give this player more touches in the game, which could result in more points for your fantasy football team.

> **Listen to the coach before the NFL season begins. But, after the season begins, there is too much at stake for the coach to always speak the truth. Ignore his chatter during the season.**

Remember those names you wrote down at the beginning of this chapter? That was your emotion talking. Are any of those names highlighted on your ranking sheet? If they are, congratulations! If they're not, congratulations! You just realized what held you back from your league's championship in the past.

4.5 - WHAT IS THE MOST IMPORTANT DRAFT POSITION?

Every fantasy football player has their own strategy and believes the most important position should be their first pick in the first round of the draft. **In reality, the most important position is the one with the largest matchup advantage.** This is not, however, the first position you will draft. But you will need to weigh this position overall as you go through each round of the draft, as I will demonstrate below.

So, go ahead and circle the position you believe is this elusive player.

Quarterback   Running Back   Wide Receiver

Tight End?   Kicker?   Defense?

Remember, this is a team sport. You would like all your positions to be strong, but there is one position that stands above all others. You must correctly choose this position and you will have little room for error.

Now, let us review the positions:

Quarterback
No doubt this is a very important position. In the NFL, he is the field general. In fantasy football, we only look at him as a point scorer. There are 32 teams in the NFL and many of them have very good quarterbacks. In your league, there are only 12 teams; therefore, your chances of getting a good quarterback are high. Many coaches will jump in the first three rounds in an effort to get the quarterback with last year's best stats. That is a huge error. You'll find plenty of good quarterbacks who score very close to the top in the sixth, seventh, and sometimes the eighth round.

Never draft a quarterback in the early rounds. Save your early rounds for other positions.

Running Back

This position is the foundation of your team. If you are going to challenge for the championship, you need at least one very strong and consistent scorer from your running backs stable. Most experts agree drafting a running back in the first round is the only way to go. I would concur. However, that does not mean drafting three running backs the first three rounds is the way to go.

There is a temptation to draft more than one running back early. Due to frequent injuries, this position will be the easiest to fill. Therefore, leaving this position to fill later and using early picks for other positions is what we call a "two-fer".

Wide Receiver

With this position, the name of the game is consistency. There are very few wide receivers that score solid points week in and week out. In fact, even the best will put up a goose egg once in awhile. If you want consistency, you only have about a half dozen good wide receivers from which to choose (look at your top WR tier). If there are 12 teams in your league and you were to get two wide receivers, then you have built a very wide gap between you and your opposition. Every year, there are three or four other wide receivers that may step up and perform well, but no one knows who they will be. You must go for your wide receivers early.

Put two of the top six wide receivers on your roster, leaving the other 11 coaches to fight for the remaining four.

Tight End

Just as with the wide receivers, it is difficult to get both consistency and high scoring with a tight end. You can definitely get consistency here – with low scores. Remember, in fantasy football the average points scored by tight ends is about four per week.

> If you want to look at the tiers for your tight ends, I believe you will find Antonio Gates in the top tier by himself (at least in 2006). Draft Antonio Gates!

2006 NEWS FLASH: Gates will be playing with a new QB. His stock now goes down (at draft time also, which is good news for you). His numbers will be down in the beginning of the season (maybe you could trade for him later). But expect him to have a strong last half of the season as the QB and Gates start to jive.

Kicker

All the experts say the kicker should be the last pick. They state you never know which kicker will be in the top for the next year. I would also concur with this. You not only can have a good kicker at the end of the draft, but during the year many will pop up on the waiver wire.

> You would prefer a kicker in a dome who also has the leg for greater than 50 yds.

Defense

In a CBS Sportsline league, a good defense will score as many fantasy football points as a good running back. In a CBS league, it is paramount to have a top defense. In many other leagues, it may not have as much importance.

> **In the CBS league, look in the fifth or sixth rounds to acquire a top defense. You should know the tendencies of your league to determine if a defense is important.**

OK, have you figured it out yet? Has your choice changed?

The most important position to draft is ... drum roll please ... the tight end position. And the only player you want at that tight end position is Antonio Gates. Gates will average in double figures on a consistent basis, while your opposition will average four points. This translates to you winning the battle between tight ends by the average margin of 8 points per weekly contest. No other position on your roster can hope to average this much of an advantage each week. Do whatever you have to do to make sure he is on your team. Find out where he is being drafted. You'll need to beat someone to the punch.

> **The tight end position is the most important position in the draft and every other owner will disregard it's advantage. No other position will give you as much of a potential advantage throughout the NFL season.**

4.6 - CHOOSING A FANTASY FOOTBALL LEAGUE

There are virtually hundreds of fantasy football leagues from which to choose. They may have similar rules or be wildly different. You will need to gauge the tendencies of how that particular league works. Your job for now, is to read the rules and look between the lines to find out how a coach can take advantage of a particular situation.

Don't expect to win the first year in a new league. The following year, lay out all your strategies to dominate.

Here are some reasons why I chose CBS Sportsline. (They are not in any particular order):

1. The prize money was about seven times the entry fee and 100 percent went to first place. Why should I share my winnings with the second-place team?

2. Trading is discouraged. This means less chance for collusion. Yes, I can make advantageous trades, but I did not want two friends teaming against me and stealing my prize money.

3. The defense scores more points than most other leagues. Many rookies coming into the CBS league don't realize this, which gives me an advantage. In fact, since they probably read that most experts say to draft a defense toward the end of the draft (and I draft the defense fairly early), they would not suspect me of being the whale that I am. Sharks and whales love playing with all the little fishes.

Find the position that scores more or less points than standard leagues and use it to your advantage.

4. You can have unlimited waiver wire pickups. (You'll learn the importance of this in Chapter 5.)

5. The draft has set parameters at positions; therefore, my opposition could not stack against me.

6. The draft itself is run very smoothly and the set up is very pleasing to the eye.

7. Data and stats were laid out in a manner conducive to my style and I referred to them often. This was very important to me.

8. Any pick ups or drops during the season were immediately forwarded to my e-mail. This meant I could track my opposition without having to go to the league site.

    Any league worth their salt should communicate with you immediately through your e-mail. Tracking your opposition is a must.

9. CBS allows you to customize the look of your home page. I customized my home page to match my strategies.

10. CBS gives you the opposition's experience in that league. Was I playing with a shark or a fish (rookie)? I like knowing my opponents.

11. In the playoff weeks, only four teams move on. This leaves less competition for the waiver wire, which, as I said before, is my strength. (Due to my 'bility). Some leagues will let the other teams continue to play even if it is not toward the championship. You're left competing with all of them for the players you may want from the community player pool.

12. My initial goal was to win my division, which meant I had to outplay only three other coaches.

4.7 - YOUR NEW BEST FRIENDS – THE ASSISTANT COACHES

In the NFL, every coach needs his assistant coaches to help him reach the championship game. You do, too. Your new best friend(s) will be critical to your success. Who are these assistant coaches?

On the Internet, they are the advice web sites. In the beginning, they will help you rank your players. During the season, they will give you good advice. You'll need more than one, as they are all set up differently and have various slants on how best to serve you. The worst they can give you is confirmation you are doing the right thing. The best they can give you is some piece of advice you would not have considered on your own.

There are hundreds (if not thousands) of advice web sites out there. You will need to find three or maybe even four sites that will give you reference points and possibly a bonus or two. A bonus is a freebie you get in addition to the normal subscription for a year's worth of advice. When comparing advice sites, the main feature I look for is the ability to e-mail my address immediately with any breaking news. They need to give me the capability to scoop my opposition. Do not use (as your main reference) your league site to gather your information. This is exactly what your opposition is reading; therefore, you will not gain an advantage. See Chapter 9 for a complete list of my favorite assistant coaches.

Assistant coaches are crucial to your success.
The best assistant coaches keep you informed of
any breaking news during any NFL week.

WARNING! All of the information is this book is based on a standard league roster and performance scoring. If you play in a non-standard league, it is your responsibility to understand how any or all of the strategies can impact your team.

SportsLine is a registered service mark of SportsLine.com, Inc. All other brand names mentioned in this book are trade- or service marks of their respective companies.

WHAT YOU WILL LEARN:

1. **The best time to draft**
2. **The best draft position**
3. **The best draft order**
4. **The one thing that will help take you to the top of the drafting class**
5. **What items to bring with you to the war room.**

Overview

The greatest joy in fantasy football is winning the championship, but the most exciting part has to be the draft. Being on a time clock and watching the other coaches draft their players is an adrenalin rush — well, at least for us couch potatoes. It is one of the easiest things to do in fantasy football, but one of the hardest to do correctly.

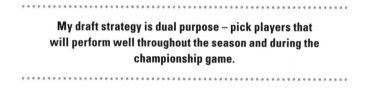

My draft strategy is dual purpose – pick players that will perform well throughout the season and during the championship game.

Consider the draft a "war room." It is where you are pitted against 11 other coaches to pick your preferred players. In this chapter, you will learn how to dominate in the war room by putting together a team that will perform well throughout the season *and* in the championship game.

5.1 - YOUR ULTIMATE WAR ROOM STRATEGY

Most experts will tell you the draft is the most important factor to a successful season. True, it is a very significant part, but you *can* overcome a weak draft. In fact, you will find only a 10 percent difference between the team with the best draft and the team with the worst. (You can't always have the very best draft, but you should strive to be in the top third.)

> **There is only an 8-point weekly advantage from the best-drafted team to the worst. You can overcome a weak draft!**

As you prepare to go into the war room, you need to remember that while the war room is very important to your opposition, to you, it is only one part of your overall planning. Let's review the four main themes of this book (not including luck) because the "big picture" is your ultimate war room strategy.

Major Strategy reporting for duty.

Training Camp

Here is where you learned the art of laying out your particular strategies. Think of this as a starting position on a football field. Having a proper training camp will put your team on the 50 yard line. That is a tremendous start for your team.

The War Room

Preparing you for the actual draft day is the framework of your team. This will take you from the 50 yd line down to your opponent's 35.

Waiver Wire Warrior

Knowing the trade desk and working the waiver wire will help you improve your team throughout the season. Now you will go from the 35 yd line, cut into the red zone, to your opponent's 15.

The Little Things That Count

Here you'll learn to compound your advantage. From the 15, to the 10, across the 5 and plunging over the goal line. TOUCHDOWN !!!!

The order of importance is the Training Camp, Waiver Wire/ Trading Desk, and, lastly, the War Room. The War Room is a one-time event, where the chips fall where they may.

Of the first three overriding themes, the war room is the least important. The experts and your opposition will disagree vehemently. Let them disagree as you dominate your way throughout the season and all the way to the championship game!

5.2 - KEEP YOUR EYE OFF THE SUPER STUDS (AND ON YOUR STRATEGY)

Everyone wants the elite point-scorers on his team at each position and will fall all over himself to draft them as early as possible. Unfortunately, no one knows the outcome of the season at the beginning.

Below is the best possible drafted team for 2005. It is not the best possible team for the championship game, but it would have served you well. Note where in the draft these particular players were picked (via CBS Sportsline and ESPN Sports), if at all. Know that every year a new top team will emerge and the average draft choice will be all over the board.

POS.	PLAYER	PTS.	CBS* AVG PICK	ESPN* AVG PICK
QB	C. Palmer	322	82nd (rd7)	76th (rd7)
RB	S. Alexander	349	6th (rd1)	2nd (rd1)
RB	L. Johnson	315	107th (rd9)	89th (rd8)
WR	S. Smith	248	62nd (rd6)	82nd (rd7)
WR	S. Moss	210	121st (rd11)	91st (rd8)
TE	A. Gates	164	47th (rd4)	35th (rd3)
K	N. Rackers	152	163rd (rd14)	undraft
DEF	Bears	268	148th (rd13)	132nd (rd11)

*Statistics from 2005.

From the above list, note several points. Filling up your team with your perceived studs has little to do with the team concept. The middle rounds are just as important as the beginning rounds, maybe more important. Look at the difference in the average picks from CBS to ESPN. You must know your league tendencies. Sometimes the only way to know is to draft more than one team from your league site and learn from live experience.

Many excellent picks will be in the later rounds. Do not lose your focus when the studs are all gone.

So while your opposition looks forward to picking their favorite stud, enjoying the NFL season, and crossing their fingers for the championship game, your role is more difficult. You must implement the strategies laid out in the previous chapters, while remaining focused on the championship and, at the same time, draft a team that will be competitive against your opposition for the 14 weeks it takes to make the playoffs.

**Many of your opposition will be drafting from the
tainted projections of the contest site. Know the tendencies
of your league.**

**In a 14-round draft, the 4th through the 9th rounds will
separate the men from the boys.**

5.3 - THE BEST TIME TO DRAFT

Most drafts take place in the few days immediately before the NFL season kicks off. The majority prefers this for one reason. While watching the preseason games, they took note of which players were injured and know to exclude them from their roster. If everybody has the same knowledge, there is no advantage for you. Remember, you want to do everything you can do, small and large, to give yourself an edge.

Schedule your draft when it is most advantageous for you. If you draft with the masses, you take a chance that the contest site's home server may crash or develop other problems. If your Internet connection is not fast, it's bound to slow way down during crunch time.

Think of it as going to Las Vegas and playing the slot machines. Some have said the slots closer to the door are looser. The reasoning behind that is, as more people walk by the door and notice more payoffs, they will step in to gamble. You would like to find a draft that is "looser." There are a couple of ways you can do this.

First, put time on your side. You would like to draft in the very earliest draft in the preseason. Every day, more information becomes available about the players in the NFL and your draft becomes a bit tighter. Pretend the draft was done in the last week of the NFL season (Week 17) and everybody had the same knowledge. There would be no question who would be a number one pick, number two and so on. The draft would be so tight you couldn't squeeze a nickel out of it. Therefore, it stands to reason the earlier you draft, the looser it will be. Most of your opposition will be drafting based on the rating sheets and how the players performed the previous year. Hopefully, you're smarter by now and have laid out a much better strategy.

The earlier the draft, the looser it tends to be.

You might fret that your stud could go down with an injury before the season even begins. That is possible; however, you have only a one in 12 chance – the same as every other coach. I would take those odds. If it does happen, you still have the rest of the NFL season to catch up. However, there is a 92 percent chance of an injury happening to one of your opposition's players. This gives you the opportunity to quickly grab his backup.

If you draft in the first week of the preseason, you'll have approximately three more weeks to watch for sleepers and gems that were never drafted. There are surprises every preseason. I guarantee that.

Take the 92 percent challenge in the very first week of preseason.

*I picked up two running backs as free agents on many of my teams in 2005. If I had waited until the last few days before the NFL season kickoff, the only way I could have gotten those players is on draft day. **Free pick ups are very rewarding.***

The earlier the draft, the longer the period for free pick ups.

The second way you can find a looser draft is to draft with the inexperienced fish (rookies). Find the leagues that are not littered with experienced coaches.

Note: The looser draft is an advantage that can quickly turn on you. Because of the possibility of poor choices by your opposition, good ranking players will fall to you early and often. You'll be like a kid in a candy store. You might be tempted to stray from your strategy. But do not fall to temptation. Stay with your strategy.

If you like shooting fish in a barrel, you'll love drafting with the inexperienced coaches.

I was told it was a FREE pickup.

5.4 - DRAFT DROPS

If you have several drafts spread out throughout the preseason, you could also take advantage of bad news from the NFL training camps. Players will fall like stones in the draft if there are any negative news stories about them. You know how those media reporters can blow up even the smallest item. As time goes by and as the NFL season is about to begin, most of the bad news about a certain player will be resolved. But in the meantime, that player could drop one-half to a full round in the actual draft. If an injury occurs (not career threatening) the drop could easily be several rounds. You will need to accurately track their draft position on a mock draft web site (see section 9.4).

Spreading out your drafts will give you a chance to draft a very valuable potential sleeper, the temporarily out of favor kind.

Preseason injuries do happen. The player could be out for a few days, a couple of weeks, or sometimes a good part of the season. Let's examine this fantasy football opportunity a bit closer. Let's say it will be an elite first-round RB who is projected to score 224 points, or an average of 14 points a game. He becomes injured in preseason and is projected to miss exactly half the season. His projected point total now can be estimated at 112 (if he can reclaim his job). You don't drop him with the other RBs who are projected at 112. The other RBs will average 7 points a game and the stud will average the same 14 when he comes back. Wow, talk about a late sleeper. If you could pick up a solid RB who will help at the end of the year, he is worth a draft pick. If he was a first-round before the injury and an eighth-round after the injury, I would look to pick him up two rounds before that. Will an injury happen just like this? Maybe not, but you need to be prepared. Because of your 'bility you have the room on your bench and the upside is worth the risk.

Preseason injuries give you three ways to improve:
free pick up of the backups, trading advantages and draft
drops. Take advantage of the early pre-season drafts.

5.5. - WHICH DRAFTING POSITION HAS THE ADVANTAGE?

Every fantasy football player has their own idea on the position from which they would like to draft, if they indeed had a choice. Unfortunately, you do not have a choice. You have to take what was given you on draft day and do your best. You must be able to put your best foot forward whether you are drafting in the 3rd position or the 11th.

Some positions are inherently better than others. Our sport is not the only one to play favorites. If you have ever played the ponies, you know most races have eight post positions from their gate. With everything else being equal, the horses in post position numbers three, four and five will win most of the races. No one knows for sure why, but it is a well-documented fact. Your fantasy football draft positions have a similar slant to them except it is not well documented. **In fact, it has never before been published.** Since you have no choice of your draft position, your job is to overcome this if given a bad hole.

ESPN stated that for 2005 the draft position for their site that won the most championships was number two. Most large fantasy football contest leagues will not give out information related to the best draft position(s), as it would only serve as a detriment to their contest growth.

In drafting from the last six spots, the odds are stacked against
you almost 2-1. You must have a strategy to overcome this.

In doing my research, I found if you want to reach the playoffs, you have a 57 percent chance if drafting from the first six spots vs a 35 percent chance from the bottom six positions. Ouch. That hurts! Were you ever depressed to find that you were stuck in hole number 11 on draft day? Well, maybe your gut feeling was warranted.

Your team will be different depending on your draft hole. Knowing this, you need to control the draft and not let the draft control you.

To overcome those odds, you must do something different to climb out of the hole. And the lessons you learned in "Training Camp" *are* something different. You are already ahead! If you draft in the first six positions, you are almost unstoppable. Some might venture to say you are on your way to dominating. For more on the draft hole, see section 10.1.

In 2005, I had the unlucky draw in the bottom six positions in 12 of my drafts. I made the playoffs in nine, for a commanding 75 percent.

Whichever hole you do the draft from, you'll want to take advantage of your position. At the very least, you need to know the average draft position of the players you covet and where you would look at obtaining them. You'll need the chart on the next page to lay out what picks you'll get. For instance, if you draft in the 10th position, you also have the 15th, the 34th, the 39th and so forth. Your team will look different than if you were to draft from, say, the second hole.

SERPENTINE DRAFT FOR 12 COACHES

SEE HOLE CHART EXAMPLE

COACHES	A	B	C	D	E	F	G	H	I	J	K	L
RD. 1	1	2	3	4	5	6	7	8	9	10	11	12
2	24	23	22	21	20	19	18	17	16	15	14	13
3	25	26	27	28	29	30	31	32	33	34	35	36
4	48	47	46	45	44	43	42	41	40	39	38	37
5	49	50	51	52	53	54	55	56	57	58	59	60
6	72	71	70	69	68	67	66	65	64	63	62	61
7	73	74	75	76	77	78	79	80	81	82	83	84
8	96	95	94	93	92	91	90	89	88	87	86	85
9	97	98	99	100	101	102	103	104	105	106	107	108
10	120	119	118	117	116	115	114	113	112	111	110	109
11	121	122	123	124	125	126	127	128	129	130	131	132
12	144	143	142	141	140	139	138	137	136	135	134	133
13	145	146	147	148	149	150	151	152	153	154	155	156
14	168	167	166	165	164	163	162	161	160	159	158	157

5.6 - PREPARE YOUR OVER/UNDER HOLE CARD

Here's a miniature cheatsheet to take with you to the war room.

Grab a sheet of paper and list in your first column, from one to 10, the rounds you want to look at. Do not list all the rounds, as the draft choices will be too varied by the end. In the second column, list your draft hole number (from the serpentine chart on page 96) to see where you will draft from in each round. The third column is the position you would prefer to draft using your strategy. The last three columns will be the players you believe will be available and that fit your drafting strategy. Some players listed in those three columns will be picked sooner than you projected and some later, hence the name "over/under."

HOLE CARD EXAMPLE:

RD	HOLE	POS	PLAYER 1	PLAYER 2	PLAYER 3
1	8	RB	Jones	Smith	Doe
2	17	WR	Smith	Bradshaw	Long
3	32	TE	XXXXX	XXXXX	XXXXX
4	41	WR	XXXXX	XXXXX	XXXXX
5	56	RB	XXXXX	XXXXX	XXXXX
6	65	DEF	XXXXX	XXXXX	XXXXX
7	80	QB	XXXXX	XXXXX	XXXXX
8	89	QB	XXXXX	XXXXX	XXXXX
9	98	WR	XXXXX	XXXXX	XXXXX
10	113	RB	XXXXX	XXXXX	XXXXX

Hey Frank. What do you get on draft day?

Again, your team will look radically different if you draft from another hole. This hole card will only help in your overall decision making and is not to be relied on as a stand-alone tool.

If you practice enough, you will be comfortable and find the winning combination(s) from any hole.

5.7 - A PERSPECTIVE ON DRAFTING FROM DIFFERENT HOLES

Believe it or not, in the war room, the war is won in the middle rounds – fourth through the ninth. Therefore, you want to be in the correct position to get the players you desire in those rounds. Every coach will have studs on their team from the early rounds and, while they are patting themselves on the back, you're just getting warmed up.

Once you know your draft hole, which for most leagues is available 24 hours in advance, you'll need to lay out your preferred players list and analyze how they match up in average draft position to your hole. That is your (over/under) hole card.

Most fantasy football players want that gold star super stud and, most likely, you are looking at only the top three to five elite RBs. If you pick first, you don't get another choice until pick 24. The coaches who do pick first will sometimes cry about not having another pick for such a long time, but, as we can see by the stats, it is a real advantage to pick early.

A beer!

My personal favorite is to pick in the middle, as many of my opposition will not pick correctly and, many times, my desired player will fall to me.

I also like the advantage in picking 3rd or 10th, as you can outplay your opponents in turning the corner. For example, in the middle of the draft, if you are picking in the 10th spot, you have the 58th pick in round 5. You'll not pick again until No. 63. That leaves four picks for your opposition. Let's say you have your sights set on a quarterback and a running back. The 11th and 12th coaches already have a quarterback and one of the coaches has no running backs at all. You take the calculated risk and choose the running back and let the quarterback fall to you on the next pick. When you analyze your opposition, you can sometimes make a sticky situation very simple.

In the war room, you need to look around the corners.

If you are unfortunate enough to get stuck with the 12th hole, don't despair. It has a built-in advantage. You'll receive the first waiver wire free-agent pick. This is like having one extra free choice over all 11 other coaches.

As the #12 coach, do not give up your extra free pick once the draft is over.

5.8 - KNOW YOUR OPPOSITION

If you know the other coaches from prior experience, you may be able to analyze who they might likely draft. For example, coach No. 7 likes to take quarterbacks early. Once you know your draft position, see if there's anything else you can find out about your opposition that could be of help. Prior experience is one way (if you kept notes). Another way is friendliness. Before the draft starts, volunteer where you are from and others in the league may respond likewise. If you find a coach drafting early from Indianapolis, there's a good chance he will take an Indianapolis player. (Keep those same notes during the season for trading.) Make that assumption and work it to your advantage.

Also, you must know which hole the coaches *in your own division* are drafting from. Winning your division is an automatic berth to the playoffs, so make sure your opposition does not get a leg up on you. If a division coach were to take Priest Holmes (2005), then I would strongly consider, if it fits my overall plans, taking Larry Johnson. If the division coach takes Peyton Manning, I would strongly consider Marvin Harrison. You must not only draft for your two goals, as stated earlier, but it's a must for you to keep one eye on the overall draft and the other eye on your division.

Watch the teams in your division and dovetail your draft with them, if possible.

5.9 - GUARANTEES ARE YOUR SECRET WEAPON

Draft with **guarantees** when it is warranted. Let's say you covet a player with an average draft position of 62 and you pick in the sixth hole. You can take a chance by waiting until the sixth round and cross your fingers. But if you want more of a *guarantee* because he is a player you feel you must have, you must be ready to take him in the fifth round. Once you have the "must" players set, you have to surround them with the best picks for your overall team. Don't be afraid to take a player earlier than his average draft position. That's all it is, an average. Your job is to land as many of your preferred players as you can and sometimes you need to use that *guaranteed* angle. The biggest risk is other coaches laughing at you for picking a player a round too early, but you know names can't hurt you, right?! Go back to section 5.2. Do you believe that the ESPN players are any smarter in choosing Antonio Gates earlier than the CBS players? Or that the CBS players were smarter than the ESPN players in choosing Steve Smith? If you could wait until around the 82nd pick (ESPN) for Steve Smith then great, but, if you wanted a lock, you could even look at pick 55 and be satisfied. The guarantees are part of your preferred player strategy and they anchor your team concept.

> **Do not be afraid to draft players early, therefore guaranteeing them on your roster.**

You can find the average draft position for each player from one of your assistant coaches, listed in section 9.4. This is great free information to have by your side.

5.10 - THE BEST DRAFT ORDER

Everybody has their own draft order strategy. Most try to follow their plan, without any flexibility. I will give you the strategy I followed in almost every one of my 21 drafts that proved very successful. If you'd like to try your own pet strategy, you'll have the opportunity to implement it with that "P" item coming up at the end of this chapter.

Here's a run down on each position:

Quarterbacks

There are many outstanding quarterbacks in the NFL who score solid points available in rounds seven, eight and even nine. Many of the other coaches, especially in 2006, will rush to take quarterbacks in the first three rounds. Let them. Every quarterback they take will push other (preferred) players down to you.

The only quarterback you should even consider in the first round (for 2006) would be Peyton Manning. Even that move would be a stretch unless you knew he was going to throw 49 touchdowns once again.

It is better to save your early draft choices for other positions and pick up your quarterbacks much later. It would be nice to choose not only the quarterbacks you have highlighted on your cheat sheet, but also <u>two</u> or three who would complement each other by playing match ups. In playing match ups, you should easily be able to score just as many points with your quarterback as somebody who drafted one in early rounds. If quarterbacks do start flying early, do not panic. Just watch the draft room. When the later rounds come, they will not be picking up a second quarterback because they have other needs; therefore, your QB choices will still be there.

In every draft, there is always some clown taking a big name QB in the first round. In one of my drafts in 2005, it must have been the convention of clowns, because in the first 15 draft picks there were 6 QBs drafted. What a run. It almost feeds itself as one coach after another panics and picks a QB. Well, I was almost beside myself, as I had ample choices for top RBs and WRs. The QB run was soon dead and I still got my QB choice at his normal spot in Round 7. Some drafts are so loose they become weird. You should be ready to change your strategy to take advantage of the clowns. You will know a weird draft in Round 1. It won't be pennies from heaven; it will be RBs from heaven.

I can predict the motion of heavenly bodies, but not the madness of crowds.

— *Isaac Newton*

Choose good quarterbacks later in the draft and play match ups.

Running Backs

Every expert believes that the running back, the foundation of your team, should be your first-round pick. However, toward the end of the first round, the other coaches start panicking and will pick a quarterback or wide receiver. That is not a smart move. They are letting their emotions take over, because they feel that, since the gold star super stud running backs are gone, they have to go to a different position. Again, I am thrilled to be playing against them.

Stay with the running back in the first round. Do not deviate. In keeping with my strategy, I won't look for my second running back until the 4th or 5th round. I can *guarantee* that, during the NFL season, you will have many, many more opportunities to get running backs and some of them will actually carry your team. You may appear weak as Week 1 begins, but the season is long and this is the easiest position to fill – by far. You must keep true to your discipline.

It's important that you understand the following tip.

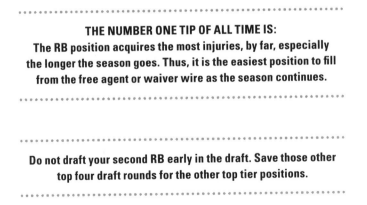

THE NUMBER ONE TIP OF ALL TIME IS:
The RB position acquires the most injuries, by far, especially the longer the season goes. Thus, it is the easiest position to fill from the free agent or waiver wire as the season continues.

Do not draft your second RB early in the draft. Save those other top four draft rounds for the other top tier positions.

Wide Receivers

There are truly only a half-dozen consistent high-scoring wide receivers in the game today. You must get one of those on your team. You need to do this in the second or early third round. If you are able to get two of the six, you'll be on your way to a championship. This is where most coaches go wrong, creating weak spots on their team all season long. Although wide receivers are the most numerous via the player pool totals, you have to look at it from the standpoint of quality. There are probably 15 quarterbacks and 15 running backs I would accept on my teams with a smile, but there are only half as many high-scoring wide receivers. Both wide receiver spots need to be strong. If you cannot get two in the beginning, you had better hope your trades or waiver wires work for you.

The top tier of WRs is about 6 deep. If you score two out of six, you make the other 11 coaches fight for the remaining four.

Don't start weak at the wide receiver position. Consistently high scoring wide receivers are the hardest to find during the NFL regular season. If you start out weak at the WR position you may end up the very same way.

Tight End

As I said in section 4.5, for a consistently high scoring tight end, there is only one – Antonio Gates. You must get him at all costs.

For the 2006 draft year, Antonio Gates will probably average in the mid-third round. If you draft in the late third round, the chances are you'll miss him. Consider grabbing him with your second pick. The other coaches will laugh their heads off, but he is the key to your team. If you don't agree with me, or you missed your opportunity, I say a sleeper in the later rounds who could perform admirably well is Todd Heap of the Baltimore Ravens.

You may panic and think using the second pick overall for a tight end is a waste. Let me explain it this way. In the first round of every draft, I drafted a running back and, in most cases, he did well for me. But, by the time the championship game arrived, I had lost my number one pick on 10 of the 12 championship teams (83 percent). (Deuce McAllister, D. Davis, and E. James). Ouch!

I still won 85 percent (12 out of 14) of my games without my number one pick. **My point is, don't worry about what pick you use, just get the players that will show up to play.** *Does this take big cajones? You bet. Not only will you have the best at this position, which is a huge advantage each week over your opposition, but you have to carry only one tight end the entire season, which fits like a glove with your 'bility. (2005)*

Drafting a player too early or having a drafted player bust will not doom your draft nor ruin your season.

Kicker

Kickers are destined to be dropped. Yes, they score points and, yes, they will help your team, but they are truly a dime a dozen. Overall, they're very equal. **You want to pick (not draft) a kicker who has the leg to kick over 50 yds** and will have good weather (or a dome) in playoff weeks. Whoever meets those criteria is your choice during the season. More information on what I mean by "pick" is in section 8.1.

Defense

As stated in section 1.2, the defense in the CBS league is worth more than some other leagues (because of the unique scoring method) and, thus, this is a very powerful position. Many of your opposing coaches won't realize this. There are two criteria: choose a good defense team that *also* has easy games during the playoffs.

Do not pick the defense that tends to go off the board in the war room first. That would push your drafting hand too hard. Look at your first tier of defenses. To most fantasy coaches, they appear equal, which may be true, but you, of course, have your "preferred" defense. Every year there is a consensus top defense that will go number one (even though they are all even in the top tier). Never select the number one pick because then you must choose that defense in the early rounds and force yourself. The draft will then control you. However, once one of the other coaches takes the number one defense, your tone is set when the rest of the tier is drafted in the next three rounds. This will allow your draft choice to fall to you. You may believe your preferred defense should go in Round 5 but, in watching the situation develop, you can sometimes wait as late as Round 7.

You are looking for the defense that may be picked, at an average, as the third or fourth off the draft board. If the defenses are not being picked early in your particular draft, you may be able to push your defensive pick down the draft board. If you do your job and pick a good defense, you have to carry only one for most of the season. Be aware – it

"PREFERRED DE-FENSE!"

is very hard to pick a good defense. In the first three weeks, there may still be some gems in the player pool that you may want to pick up and watch as they develop. A good defense at CBS SportsLine will score as many, if not more, points than your running back position.

Ignore the consensus #1 defense and let the 3rd or 4th best defense fall to your draft hole.

If you use your 'bility (see section 4.2), you'll have only one kicker, one tight end and one defense to start the season. This will give you the 'bility for your bench to dominate.

5.11 - THE "P" ITEM

You must know how the draft will unfold in the later rounds. What round will the third tier of wide receivers still be available? When will the third defense you want be gone? When will the ninth quarterback go off the board? Knowing the answers to the above will let you plan your strategy in two ways. First, you will know when to choose that player in order to guarantee he will be a part of your team. Secondly, you won't panic during your 90 seconds on the button.

How will you be able to answer these questions and stay cool under pressure? Practice, practice, and more practice. Do not skimp here. If you do, all of training camp will go down the tubes.

Practice with the Draft Dominator until you are very comfortable with the software and can draft from any hole successfully.

There are web sites where you can practice against other real players for live drafts (MockDraftCentral.com). The negative aspect of this situation is you would have to wait for them to show up. I believe ESPN has a practice site where you can go up against the computer. That is not all bad. I recommend downloading drafting software onto your computer. I found an excellent one at FootballGuys.com. While it is not the only one, it's the one with which I have personal experience. This software has taken my draft skills and honed them to a highly tuned machine, regardless of what hole I am drafting from. The best way to describe the software is "dynamic." The name of this software is the "Draft Dominator."

You can play with the Draft Dominator all day and night, from any hole you want. You can vary your strategies on who you want to draft, force your opposition to take different players, and watch how the draft will unfold. At the end of each draft, you'll be measured (point system) to see how your team compares to others. If your team does not measure up, don't rationalize or make excuses. Find ways to improve your team. When I practiced, I took the best available player to raise my grade. I then went back and snuck in some of my preferred players. After much practice, I found out what combinations worked. I did this from every hole, as the draft changes depending on your position.

One negative aspect of the Draft Dominator is that every draft is very tight, which does not mimic the real drafts. This negative is actually a plus, because you will blow away the other coaches in the real world. If you can score a high grade with a tight draft, you'll be on top of your draft with a looser one. In the real world, if you play your cards right, most of your drafts will be loose. But, every once in awhile, you'll have a tight draft and have to fight tooth and nail to come out on top.

Let's review some of the other features of the Draft Dominator.

The program is easy to download and install, and allows you to import all the NFL players and their latest projections, as well as update these as the season progresses. You can personalize the interface to fit your needs and, in your case, specific strategies. For coaches playing in different leagues, it allows you to save several set ups according to the various rules and parameters of those leagues.

Most of the information is on one screen in front you. First, there is your player pool. In this player pool, you'll have the average draft position (make sure you do a download just before the draft), the projected points, and the VBD. The VBD is your secret weapon. I will explain this in more detail in just a moment. You also have the draft status as the rounds unfold, the team stats, which are very important in watching your opposition fill the roster, and the team rosters themselves. Having all this information and changing what you want to look at with a click of the mouse will give you a very relaxed and enjoyable draft.

Note: You'll need an estimated total of eight hours to be very comfortable with the program and very good at drafting.

5.12 - THE VBD (VALUE BASED DRAFTING)

The VBD is dynamic in its application and should be used congruently with your strategies.

Many experts believe this is now the only way to draft. Similar tools may be available under different names, but the one I used was included with the Draft Dominator software. When you download the software, you need to read the instructions for more detail. They have taken the player pool and its projections, applied their mathematical formulas to find baselines, and then performed measurements off of those baselines. This will tell you if it is better to draft the third wide receiver or the eighth running back. It tries to make an "apples vs oranges" comparison more of an "apples vs apples" comparison. It does not look at your team's needs, as it is only looking at the player pool itself. As the player pool depletes, the mathematical formulas change. You can even click on something they call "best value pick" and it will show you, via the VBD math, who you should strongly consider. Be forewarned, this VBD method can't be used for the entire draft. Toward the end of the draft, you must be primarily concerned with your own roster and not the overall player pool.

When the actual live draft is at hand, you will run this program at the very same time and populate it manually with the live draft. There is a huge advantage running this program simultaneously with the live draft. It will give you the ability to "out think" your opposition. It will not slow you down, but will enhance your experience.

Personalize the Draft Dominator software to your league; otherwise, its results will be tainted against you.

5.13 - DRAFT STRATEGY 101

Now that you have read the nuts and bolts of my war room strategy, let's put the first few rounds on paper.

Round 1

You: RB1 – Always choose a running back. Most of the time, he will be from your preferred list. You should have about three running backs on your list: one for the beginning-third of the draft, one for in the middle and one for the end. If the one in the middle would fall to you toward the end, more power to you.

Opposition: Seven coaches will take RBs, a couple will take QBs, and a couple will take WRs.

Round 2

You: WR – You must assure yourself of grabbing one of the top six, excluding the problem players.

Opposition: Most will take RBs, but some will grab WRs and an occasional QB.

Round 3

You: TE – I understand how this hurts now, but a little pain will be more gain. With my drafting strategy, it's actually harder to find another tight end later in the draft and you'll be looking in Round 9, when all that is left is chaff as far as the tight end position goes.

Opposition: For the most part, they will be very solid on RBs and WRs. They will end up with one of these combinations:

QB, RB, WR **or** 2 RB, WR **or** RB, 2 WR

If they go with the last choice, take note and watch them carefully. They have definitely figured out one of the secrets of the draft and are a force to be reckoned with.

Round 4

You: Get the second wide receiver from the top six in your first tier (of WRs) and you'll have your opposition sucking wind (although they will not have a clue as of yet). If unavailable, take your best RB.

Opposition: Will be jumping for the quarterback and the second tier of wide receivers because their running backs are mostly full.

Round 5

You: Depends on the previous pick. If I got my wide receiver in the fourth round, I would concentrate on a running back here. RBs are slim, but I would take the best available RB. If I got a RB in the previous round, I would look at guaranteeing my defense. By taking the defense now, I have freedom in the next round to move up my quarterbacks, if necessary. In the next round, one of the RBs may also fall to me. Therefore, it is decision time. I usually do not look at a wide receiver because the bottom of tier 2 is pretty close to the top of tier 3 and I can get a tier 3 in the ninth round. As long as you know what to expect in the future rounds, it will keep you from panicking.

Opposition: They will be jumping all around and just filling their holes. After four rounds, their strategy is at an end. For the most part, you can pretty much predict who they will take. They got their studs in the first three rounds and are very happy. However, they will not be happy in the championship game.

Summary of Draft Order

Round 1	RB1
Round 2	WR1
Round 3	TE1
Round 4	WR2 if top 6 or best RB2
Round 5	RB2 or DEF1
Round 6	Whichever Round 5 did not produce
Round 7	QB1
Round 8	QB2
Round 9	best available

If I don't select a second wide receiver by Round 4, I usually wait to pick up whatever is left in Round 9 or later. They are all very similar in their tier and it doesn't hurt to wait.

Also for 2005, it seemed that if I was drafting in the bottom six holes, I was more likely to fill my team the way I wanted, but, of course, I didn't have a chance for a super stud running back.

You may want to switch a few things around, but I will state this: The tight end, defense and quarterback angles are crucial for your draft. If your league's coaches are clowns and some extra-good player drops to you, be very careful jumping on that player vs. staying true to your strategy. It will happen at some point and you then have 90 seconds to make a decision. Prepare for that.

Can you juggle?

In the war room, you must be ready to combine all your skills and knowledge and focus for about two hours to come out on top. Before you pick a player you need to look at (in no particular order)

1. Your hole possibilities for players
2. Tier boxes…to empty them or switch to another position
3. Average draft position of players
4. How your division playmates are building their teams
5. Control the draft or let it fall to you
6. Your hole possibilities for advantages over other coaches
7. The # 1 rule
8. The home field advantage
9. Dropkick (see section 8.1)
10. Your preferred players
11. Your team needs at any certain point
12. The VBD player pick
13. Your guaranteed player(s)
14. The QB match up combo

You will find that one strategy may have to override another. Also, you may need to switch strategies more than once during the draft because you cannot control what 11 other coaches are doing. If you're prepared and practiced, this is not as hard as it looks. The first thing I always do when I'm on the clock is have the BAP (best available player) picked, put him on reserve and, if the clock goes down to the last few seconds, I will draft him in my panic. In the war room, you can't waste even one round!

Okay. Now throw me the flaming sword.

Sometimes you will control the draft and sometimes you will let the draft fall to you, but never let the draft control you.

When you know both your draft date and your draft hole, instantly pull out the Draft Dominator and practice two more drafts, just to be comfortable before the live draft.

5.14 - YOUR ARSENAL

Have these materials in front of you in the war room:

1. Two untouched ranking sheets, from which your opposition may be basing their decisions, to be used as a reference guide. One of those should be from the contest web site itself. This is for reference only.
2. A current list of average draft picks (from the Draft Dominator). (Or see section 9.4 for web sites on ADP)

3. Your personalized over/under hole card

4. Your colored-coded customized cheatsheet of preferred players

5. The Draft Dominator, which will be set up ahead of the draft with all 12 team names and the proper parameters. Any team also in your division will have the initials "DP" next to their name. This means "division player" and will keep you aware of your opposition, who is your most direct competition.

The pre-training and the war room are now complete and you are ready to take your team down into the red zone. See you on the Waiver Wire!

WARNING! All of the information is this book is based on a standard league roster and performance scoring. If you play in a non-standard league, it is your responsibility to understand how any or all of the strategies can impact your team.

SportsLine is a registered service mark of SportsLine.com, Inc. All other brand names mentioned in this book are trade- or service marks of their respective companies.

CHAPTER 6

WHAT YOU WILL LEARN:

1. Which three factors impact championship teams
2. How to best use the waiver wire to improve your team
3. How to pick up free agents
4. Why the RBs are gold
5. The role of the spotter
6. How to maximize your assistant coaches

Overview

Many fantasy football coaches approach the waiver wire work as a necessary evil, but not an essential tool to their team's success. In truth, the waiver wire will be an indispensable part of building your championship team. And if used correctly and diligently, in conjunction with all of the strategies you've implemented thus far, it will give you the greatest potential to improve your team over the course of the NFL season.

6.1 - HOW IMPORTANT IS THE WAIVER WIRE?

To demonstrate, we'll start out with a little review quiz.

Question: Out of 14 players, circle the number of players below that you believe a coach should keep if he started out with a good, solid team: (Hint: I already told you the answer in a previous chapter).

14	13	12	11	10	9	8
7	6	5	4	3	2	1

Answer: 6, 7 or 8. The average for all teams is approximately 50 percent. If you had a very poor draft, the number *remaining* would probably be lower. The moral is, if a team had little turnover, it was, for the most part, unsuccessful. Up to one-half of your team needs to be replaced for one purpose only – to improve your team as the year continues. If you are not improving your team, I can guarantee you'll be falling behind the coaches that are.

> **The facts show that the waiver wire/free agency is indispensable to a team's improvement. You desire a 50 percent annual turnover rate for your success.**

I have found the following three factors that have a huge impact on building a championship team:

Factor 1: Your draft position. Your draft position will dictate whether you will be in the **top** (first 6 holes) or **bottom** (last 6 holes) group. We have discovered that drafting in the first six positions gives you almost a two to one advantage in making the playoffs.

Factor 2: The success of your draft. Having a very good draft gives you a 60 percent greater opportunity for a winning record. Having a "very good draft" is subjective and can be broken down by grades. The grades will run from the highest (A) to the lowest (E). "A" and "B" are **excellent** drafts. A grade of "C" is an **average** draft and a grade of "D" or "E" is a **bad** draft. Every draft is graded within its own league so they naturally have a built-in bias or "curve", as you will. There are no comparisons between leagues.

Factor 3: The amount of time you use the waiver wire. On a quantitative basis only, if you are in the top third of your league in using the waiver wire, you have a 59 percent greater chance of finishing with a winning record. That advantage diminishes to 31 percent from the bottom third.

Once again, this is strictly quantitative. How many players did you pick up (free agent or waiver wire) from the player pool during the fantasy football regular season? Of the 12 coaches in your league, you will be in the **top, middle, or bottom third**. Remember, this does not compare one league to another.

You can read an in-depth analysis of these three factors in section 10.1, but let's do some comparisons and lay out some of the ground rules now. In the following chart, I break down the three factors to show the success rates. Success is defined by victories during the season. More precisely, we are searching for at least eight wins, as this amount would put your team in the playoffs the majority of the time.

The big question? What percent of teams had eight or more wins with any of these combinations?

DRAFT POSITION	DRAFT GRADE	WAIVER WORK	8 WINS OR MORE
Top	Excellent	Top	75%
Top	Excellent	Bottom	52%

A 31percent decline just for not doing your waiver work!

DRAFT POSITION	DRAFT GRADE	WAIVER WORK	8 WINS OR MORE
Bottom	Bad	Top	37%
Bottom	Bad	Bottom	16%

A 57 percent decline. You are hurting yourself if you're not active on the wire.

DRAFT POSITION	DRAFT GRADE	WAIVER WORK	8 WINS OR MORE
Top	Bad	Top	33%
Bottom	Average	Top	66%
Top	Average	Bottom	52%

We can mix and match these three configurations all day long, but I believe this lays out the importance of the waiver wire. You must not only scour, but mine the waiver and free agent wire. The war room is a one-time event, but your waiver/free agent crop needs to be harvested weekly. It is the best way to improve your team throughout the season.

Note: Don't use the waiver wire willy-nilly, just to increase your stats. You have a responsibility to your team to make a move only if you can prove to yourself that the pick up and corresponding drop will fill a need on your team. All teams coming out of the war room will have warts. Warts are weak positions on a team. Your job during the season is to make your team as close to wart-free as possible.

6.2 - HOW DOES THE WAIVER WIRE WORK?

It is crucial you find the different ways of harvesting the player pool for your team's improvement. Many leagues have different rules when it comes to the waiver wire. You'll need to find out how your league's waiver wire will impact your weekly decisions.

Look Coach, I'm on the Waiver Wire.

At kickoff of the first game of each week, all players not on a team will be locked down in what we call the "player pool." They aren't available for any team until the lock has been taken off. Usually, the lock down begins with your first NFL Sunday game but, in some weeks, the first NFL game will be on a Thursday (there will be more Thursday games in 2006). At any rate, they are locked in the player pool until Wednesday morning at approximately 2:30 a.m. eastern time. At that time, they will be released on the waiver wire to be picked up on a worst-to-first basis.

During the lock-down period, every coach has the opportunity to "apply" for any player they want to pick up for their team. Of course, for every player you pick up, you will also need to drop one, as your roster can never exceed the league limit. If more than one coach "applies" for the same player, the team with the worst record will be awarded that player. If you chose, you can "apply" for as many players as your heart desires. However, every player that you are awarded drops you to the bottom of the worst-to-first list for that particular week.

Use the lock-down player pool time for your team's advantage.

Now, here comes the tricky part. Any player not picked or not newly dropped will be a free agent that you can grab at any time without waiting in any line. Picking up a player with no restrictions whatsoever is golden. Also, any player newly dropped has to go through a 48-hour lock-down period and is again available on a new worst-to-first list. Therefore, a player dropped on Wednesday would not be available again until Friday.

The worst-to-first method (which resets every week) is the league's way of making a bad team more competitive for the league. A bad team can improve very easily with the waiver wire and there is nothing a good team can do but look on. That's exactly why you don't see teams with a record of 14-0 or teams with a record of 0-14. It is too hard to either win or lose all your games with a system that has been built to help the worst.

Let's look at an example:

Sample League Record after Week 1:

Team	Record	Points
A	1 - 0	77
B	0 - 1	94
C	0 - 1	42
D	1 - 0	66
E	1 - 0	121
F	1 - 0	83
G	0 - 1	84
H	0 - 1	69
I (you)	0 - 1	71
J	1 - 0	101
K	1 - 0	97
L	0 - 1	77

Ignoring ties, there will be six winners and six losers. (Kind of like that "50 percent rule" I keep referring to.) Without any advantage whatsoever, one team is a coin flip over another team. "Without any advantage" should never be a description for any of your teams. After Week 1, you can see that the first waiver pick will go to Team C and the last waiver choice will go to Team E. Your team (I) will have a choice available at pick number three.

> In a typical week, there may be as many "good" players dropped as there are "good" players in the entire player pool.

You, however, want to play a game inside a game. You're interested in a player you highly believe no other coach will even consider, at least at this time. You can practically guarantee you will grab your player by putting him on your waiver wire **or** you can hope he will be available later as a free agent and, at the same time, protect (and improve) your current waiver position. You go for the latter.

Even though in the real world you can't see what your opposition is doing until after the waiver wire is finished, I'll lay out a possible scenario for you to view here.

Wed. Waiver Wire Order	Wednesday Pickup	Wednesday Drop	New Friday Waiver Wire Order
T-C	RB	KICKER	T-I (you)
T-H	WR	W, Dunn	T-L
T-I (you)	NONE		T-G
T-L	NONE		T-A
T-G	NONE		T-F
T-B	QB	INJ RB	T-C
T-D	DEF	DEF	T-H
T-A	NONE		T-B
T-F	NONE		T-D
T-K	TE	WR	T-K
T-J	QB	QB	T-J
T-E	RB	DEF	T-E

The free agent pool after the Wednesday waiver wire still had your man available and you went immediately and picked him up. However, locked-on waivers until Friday morning were (Column 3): KICKER, W. Dunn, INJ RB, DEF, WR, QB, DEF.

Did you notice that since you didn't pick up a player in the first waiver of the week that you now moved up to the first position of the second waiver of the week? Sometimes, if you don't see an immediate improvement for your team with the first waiver wire, sit back (and climb positions) and watch who gets dropped. You might be very surprised which players some coaches give up on. It happens quite often. In this case, you would jump on W Dunn on the second waiver wire of the week.

Try to climb the waiver list as the week goes on, if possible.

In a typical waiver wire week, you'll find your position will increase by about six spots if you don't participate in the first waiver wire for the week. Later in the year, as other coaches lose their interest or their focus, there will be less activity and you will jump fewer spots. Pay attention to your league tendencies.

In some cases, more than one coach will want the same player on the waiver wire. You must determine how badly you also want this particular player. Is it worth losing your waiver position? Only you can decide.

The free agency should be used for the players you see useful down the road. Most coaches only look one week ahead. You can pick up players several weeks ahead, for free, because the others have not even considered them yet. Don't forget to get information about free agents from your assistant coaches. News can come at any time of the day and any day of the week. Be ready to jump because, as everyone knows, free is always good.

A free agent is a gift from the fantasy football gods.

Using your first waiver wire as an automatic is a waste of your league-given power. It is always smarter to use the free agency and intertwine this with your waiver wire strategy. You must pick and choose which way to go each week and with each league.

Another trait of winning coaches is the greater use of the free agents, as opposed to the use of the waiver wire. I don't know if this truly matters but, whichever way you choose to go, you'll need to be active. Use every angle to develop your team, even if it's only a possibility of improvement. Your goal is to raid that player pool or harvest that crop. **Become the waiver wire warrior.**

6.3 - WHY MINE THE WAIVER WIRE?

Do you want more proof that harvesting your player crop works? Let's look at it from a different viewpoint. Every week there are six winners and six losers (excluding ties). Below is my League Improvement Summary Chart, I've examined "All" teams, "Winners", and my personal teams' scores for the first seven weeks and the last seven weeks to determine the percentage of improvement over the year. This will show the gains for each category. For the complete League Improvement Chart see section 10.2.

AVERAGE FOR 14 WEEKS OF THE SEASON			
	A **SCORES** **1ST 7 WKS**	**B** **SCORES** **2ND 7 WKS**	**POINTS** **IMPROVED**
ALL COACHES	83.2	83.4	0.19
WINNERS ONLY	94.8	96.1	1.30
MY 21 TEAMS	87.1	105.0	17.83

Look at the average scores for the "All" and "Winning" teams and compare them to the gains for my teams. Most fantasy football coaches are only looking to win that week and are not focused on the improvement of their team as the season progresses. This is not drop-dead proof as there are far too many variables but, again, it shows you the trend.

**Mining the player pool greatly increases your potential
and enhances your playoff odds.**

6.4 - HOW TO MINE FOR THE BEST PLAYERS

Before you read this section, remember: your 'bility gives you the extra spots on your roster – use them!

Running Backs

Much of the strategy for this book is counter to conventional fantasy football strategies for the RB position. For example, 90 percent of the fantasy football experts tell you to draft all the RBs you can and/or as early as you can. However, I told you to focus on a stud RB only in the first round, and then look elsewhere. Why would I tell you to start the season with a weak second RB? Because you don't play the championship game until Week 16.

Remember the 'bility from section 4.2? The waiver wire is where it comes into play. The 'bility gives you many roster spots to fill the needs of your particular team but, without hesitation, you should always consider the running backs first and foremost. Too many running backs is a great dilemma to have. It means a greater chance at that elusive star stud, greater control over your league and greater chances to dominate. It literally becomes a "rack'em and stack'em" mentality. Who? Why? When? How many?

**How many RBs should you have on your team?
As many as you can fit on your roster.**

For a roster of 14 players, having six RBs is not out of line. You won't have six immediately, but will build toward that. Your goal is to have more point-scoring RBs on your team than anyone else in your league.

Why?

1. You will force the other coaches to come through *you* for their RB needs. That's a powerful position to be in. Every coach covets two strong RBs each and every week. Who knows, maybe a trade could benefit your team?

2. The high injury rate. As discussed previously, RBs have the highest injury rate and, thus, they have the greatest impact for or against your team. As the number of available RBs drops over the season due to injuries, you'll have more RBs than your opposition and, therefore the greatest potential to improve as the season wears on.

3. You will increase your ability to play match up from week to week.

4. A RB has the potential to touch the ball 20 to 30 times a game. Thus, they have the highest potential to score points for your team. They say he who has the gold rules. In fantasy football, he who has the RBs has the gold.

5. Any RB you put on your team is a solid "two-fer." Which means while he may or may not play for you, he *definitely* won't play against you. He could also be a "three-fer" – he plays for *you*, not for the coach whose starter he replaced, and not for the coach who would have picked him on the waiver wire if he'd had the opportunity. You get stronger while the rest of your league gets weaker. You gotta love it!

**The RB position is the easiest to play match up with
and increase your point potential.**

Who?

1. RBs on the depth list. If you hear even a slight whisper of an RB moving up on his NFL team's depth list (for whatever reason), then run over the women and children to pick up this player. Do it quickly, before he is a known commodity; otherwise, you'll be competing against the 11 other coaches.

2. When a RB is injured, look to his backup. Even if the prognosis of the injury is slight and they project he will be out for only a week, watch out. One week can easily turn into four to five weeks.

3. Back ups on teams that won't make the playoffs. As the season continues, look for back up RBs on teams that won't be making the playoffs or are just plain quitting on the season. Those teams may want to give some other players a look-see for next year. Watch for a RB with an increasing percentage of carries over the course of a few games.

4. During the latter weeks, look at your own handcuff situation.

5. Possible gems. The majority of the NFL teams will not have their starting RB (for various reasons) play the entire year. So watch for the occasional gems waiting in the wings. Then snag them.

**Find the NFL stats not printed in your daily newspaper.
Those untold stories can be future gems forming.**

When?

1. Whenever the opportunity presents itself. Always be on the look out for a great RB can come at any time during the season, week and even the day.

2. When your assistant coaches say so. The job of your assistant coaches is to give you the information the public (and most of your opposition) does not have.

   Check with your assistant coaches early and often so you can pounce on any players before the other coaches have sniffed anything. Case in point – search the data for the number of times a particular wide receiver was thrown to. The newspapers may report this receiver had three catches and 42 yards receiving. Not anything impressive. But your assistant coaches will tell you this wide receiver was thrown to 14 times. If the NFL coach and the quarterback have that much confidence in this wide receiver, then possibly you should have confidence in putting him on your team.

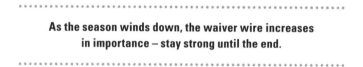

As the season winds down, the waiver wire increases in importance – stay strong until the end.

3. After the NFL Week 10. Injuries crop up around this time and new RB possibilities are literally falling from the trees. You'll be shocked. You'll also have less competition during this time, as many of the other coaches are out of the playoffs and have lost interest.

4. During the playoffs. **You must scarf up any and all RB possibilities, not so much for yourself, but to keep them from your opponent.** At the playoffs, you are playing your "two-fer" hand straight up. What you get, they don't. Simple as that.

5. If you want to be sneaky. On the Sunday before the games begin, look at your next week's opponent (or look two weeks ahead, if you're feeling extra sneaky). What would happen if his RB were injured on Sunday? His backup would be an instant celebrity on the Wednesday waiver wire, especially if his team played a poor defensive team in the next week or two. Why not grab that backup now, before lock down, just on a whim? If the starting RB doesn't acquire an injury, just drop the backup RB and, more than likely, you'll be able to pick up the player you dropped before on free agency and be no worse off. But, if he is injured, you'd have your opponent in a huge hole for that game.

6. If a RB has even a slight positive rumor. Drop your lowest player (spotter) and pick up the one with the buzz and watch things develop. If nothing happens, drop him on Saturday or Sunday and go back to your other player, if he cleared the waivers.

> **The early bird gets the running back. Stack them up on your roster on the earliest whisper you hear.**

7. When there's a late scratch. Before Sunday's game time, you'll find a player who warmed up with his team but was a late scratch. Jump on his backup as soon as possible. **Always have a spotter on your team** – a player that can be dropped if you need a quick pick up. At this juncture, seconds matter. Don't worry about correcting your team; you'll still have some time left to update your own roster.

> **Have a "spotter" already named on your roster for quick decision making, particularly the 30 minutes before kickoff on Sunday.**

8. Know your league tendencies in order to recognize when to hand-cuff your own RB studs and **then do it two weeks earlier.**

Defense

During the first two to three weeks, find a defense on the waiver that is performing well and put that defense on your bench. Watch the D for a couple of weeks and see which defense you wish to use for the rest of the season.

Let's say you have a solid defense but, in two weeks, you'll be going against the league's highest point team. There could be an average defense still out in the player pool that will be playing against a very weak team in that particular week. Okay, so you have to carry two defenses for a couple of weeks. The possible reward is worth the risk.

Wide Receivers

In the beginning of the NFL season, it is difficult to pick up quality wide receivers. (That is why you'll follow my strategy in Chapter 4 and pick up the strongest wide receivers you can get.) Should you need to replace your wide receivers, there's an excellent chance of picking them up later in the season, after they've shown their true colors and look to have favorable match ups. The wide receivers I pick up as the season progresses

are the ones who are thrown to frequently, though their stats may not show many catches. If a quarterback keeps throwing his way and shows a pattern each week, eventually they're going to be on the same page. It might be worth a roster spot.

Playing match up is not the preferred method for wide receivers, but it can fill holes in your roster late in the season.

Wonder Kids

Now, let's discuss who you don't want to pick up. Many weeks, especially in the early part of the NFL season, there will be a player (non-RB) who will have a huge stat line, usually a QB or a WR. The truth of the matter is they will not do that again and, in fact, will crawl back underneath the rock from whence they came. But all the coaches will line up on the waiver wire for this new wonder kid, only to be disappointed in the coming weeks. Don't get in line, but do watch who has been dropped because of the new wonder kid and consider getting in *that* line.

Don't chase one-week flukes or wonder kids on your waiver wire.

Other "Insider" Info

After the NFL season begins, you'll be able to pick up from the player pool from Wednesday until Sunday kickoff each and every week. If you do your draft in the first week of preseason, you'll have three to four weeks to pick up players as free agents. The preseason is a smorgasbord. Have fun!

Most other coaches do not plan ahead. Therefore, if you can be a week or two ahead in your planning and have the extra roster spots to spare, you can clean up your warts for your team or create warts in your opposition's team (whoever you'll play that particular week).

From Week 10 on, refocus your energy on the waiver wire because other coaches will have given up or lost their focus.

As I said when referring to RBs, you'll see NFL teams giving up around the 10th or 11th week. The same thing happens in your own league as some of your opposition has grown weary and is not paying very close attention to the waiver wire. Use this to your advantage.

This next strategy may not get you excited, but it was one that helped me to dominate. As I mentioned earlier, the waiver wire takes place on Wednesday morning at 2:30 a.m. eastern time and takes about 10 seconds. After the waiver wire is over, anyone can pick up free agents from the player pool. Your opposition may want to pick from the free agency and, when he gets up at 7:00 in the morning, he'll start his search.

That coach (or 10 other coaches) may have the same players in mind you do. Therefore, you need to get up on Wednesday morning at 3:00 a.m. and snatch your free agents from the player pool. Once the other coaches do the search and learn their picks are long gone, they will scratch their heads, utter a four-letter word, and go to work. You scooped them!

Wake up early every week, while your opposition sleeps, and exercise your constitutional right to free agency.

The whole point of the waiver wire is to improve your team for your championship game. 70 percent of your research time is on the player pool, 20 percent is on trades and the remaining 10 percent is on your team. Why so little on your team? Because no one can touch any of your players unless you allow them to.

Yes, you may have short-term player pick ups to help you win in a particular week. That short-term player may turn out to be a long-term player. You'll have the entire season to clean up the warts for your team and the waiver wire was made just to do that. You must measure your improvement as the season goes on. At this stage of the game, the coach who can eat, sleep, and breathe fantasy football will be rewarded.

WARNING! All of the information is this book is based on a standard league roster and performance scoring. If you play in a non-standard league, it is your responsibility to understand how any or all of the strategies can impact your team.

SportsLine is a registered service mark of SportsLine.com, Inc. All other brand names mentioned in this book are trade- or service marks of their respective companies.

CHAPTER 7

THE TRADING DESK:
Trade Your Way to the Championship

WHAT YOU WILL LEARN:

1. How to find and make the perfect trade
2. The four main trading rules
3. How to keep your long-term strategies intact
4. How to take advantage of inexperienced coaches
5. When to risk making division rivals

Overview

Trading is one of the most enjoyable elements of the fantasy football experience. When you make a trade, you put your personal stamp of value on the players and negotiate with the other coaches every week. The very act of trading taps into an almost primal barter-type instinct that motivates us to go out and conquer our little corner of the world.

The waiver wire is used to drop a poor player for a better player. Trades are used in a win-win situation.

In reality though, trading is the poorer cousin to the waiver wire in improving your fantasy football team. As you learned in Chapter Six, every team has warts and it's your job to clean them up throughout the season. On the waiver wire, however, you are giving up a poor player for a better player. In trading, you must, in some form of valued terms, give up a good player to get a good player. Yes, trading can help, but I don't recommend spending a great deal of time working this system. That said, this chapter will help you learn the basics of trading and how to maximize the fun *and* potential of each trade you make.

7.1 - THE PROCESS

The process of the trade is really a check and balance system. First, you will make an offer to trade one of your players for another player on a different coach's team. If the coach accepts your offer, it will go to the remaining coaches in your league and they will cast a vote to allow or veto the trade. If they allow the trade, it is processed immediately. However, if enough coaches agree the trade isn't in the best interest of all parties, they will veto the trade. The veto does not scuttle the trade; it only sends the transaction up to the next level, placing it on the desk of your commissioner.

At the beginning of the season, all of the coaches in a league elect a commissioner. The commissioner is empowered to take all vetoed trades and, after weighing all relevant information, renders their decision. What he or she says, goes. If he says "yes," the trade is consummated immediately. If it is rejected, the whole transaction is sent back to the beginning. A trade is more likely to be approved if the exchange value appears equal.

Behold, the power of ME.

Note: Because of inherent conflicts of interest, it is best if the commissioner you elect is not another coach in your league, but many smaller leagues work that way.

What constitutes an equal trade?

A trade involving two players of the same value constitutes an equal trade. Therein lies the problem, or the opportunity, depending on how you look at it. Each individual coach places his or her own value on each player, and most every coach has his or her own method of valuation. Thus, "the same value" is relative. A particular player that you believe is very good may be terrible in another coach's eyes. Or vice versa. Don't assume – and this is a good thing – that any coach agrees with your value system. On each trade, you'll need to discern what the other coach values. If your opponent truly believes he is trading away a "lesser" player and receiving a "better" player, he sees that as a victory.

> **A perfect trade is when your opponent "thinks" he has received the better value, but you "know" you did.**

In many cases, at least on the surface, you are trading equals so your team remains virtually the same. You never want to make tons of trades or trade just for the sake of trading. Remember, 50 percent of trades won't work out and 50 percent will – that old 50/50 rule crops up again. Trading your players does involve some risk, but no more risk than just holding on to your same players. Risk is not mitigated in, either way. We all would love to brag about the players we just traded away who then get injured and are out for the season. However, the reverse could occur with your player or the player you decided not to trade. Luck knows no boundaries.

> **After the season begins, point projections do not determine the "proper value" of any particular player. Projections, after all, are only projections.**

If trading is to be fair, it must be advantageous to both teams. It needs to be a win-win situation. If you take unfair advantage of an unsuspecting coach, you'll likely never be able to make another trade in that league again, as the other coaches may blackball you. Trades can come in many different flavors and it should always serve to benefit both parties.

7.2 - THE LEAGUE'S ROLE

Throughout this book, I have preached the need to know your own league's rules, scoring, tendencies and even history. If you want to be the best, you'll want to find advantages from these four areas.

Here's a quick lesson on a few rules. Every league has their own roster limit. You can be under the roster limit but you cannot be over – or can you? If you make a trade of one player from your roster for three players from your opposition's and the trade is approved, then you would be two over the limit. Some leagues would force you to drop two players before the trade is consummated. At CBS SportsLine, you are allowed to be over the roster limit until the kickoff on the Sunday game (if there is no Thursday game). By kickoff, you must reduce your roster but, for the week, you had two extra players and – even better – time to decide your strategy with no interference from other coaches.

That may not seem huge, but suppose you traded a one-for-three in preseason and had three to four weeks of two extra players over your opposition? Hmmm... The point is, all leagues have their own rules to abide by. Do your research and seek out advantages to give you more possibilities.

Here's an example of a league tendency from one of my past leagues. In 2004, I offered a trade to my opposition of an RB for an RB and, to sweeten the pot, I threw in a junk player of mine I was planning to drop anyway. I figured maybe two-for-one might help swing him over. He accepted. The trade then was vetoed and was sent to the commissioner. Everything then remained status quo – for a week! While the commissioner weighed his decision, my players were locked. My junk player, who I would have dropped, kept me from using a roster spot for a full week. And in the end, the commissioner rejected the trade offer.

I learned my lesson and, in 2005, I thought I would do the reverse. I made an offer to my opposition asking that he give me a junk player with the normal trade, which would cause his player to be locked for a week. Of course, 2005 was the year my league's commissioners got their act together and decided on trades in a timelier manner. However, the moral is, even though that tiny advantage was no longer valid, I was always on the watch for even the smallest leverage.

7.3 - WHERE DO YOU STAND?

During the draft, you had your list of preferred players. Some you got, but most you did not. Now you have a second chance to land those players. Don't become obvious and tip your hand, but watch for those players, especially when they have some low scores for the week, then pounce while their value is low. By no means forget your own preferred players and trade them away after you strategized to get them in the first place.

> **The trading desk gives you a second chance to acquire your preferred player.**

Even though you started playing match up during the draft, most of the other teams (if they have the 'bility) will now be looking at match ups. As the season wears on, the SOS (strength of schedule) for the NFL teams becomes more important. Every week that passes will give your assistant coaches more information to project the future. Periodically check the SOS for changes that may benefit you.

I suggest a counting system to keep things simple. Think of the Vegas game of blackjack. There are card counters out there and they count +1 for certain cards and -1 for other cards. Whenever the remaining deck (yet to be dealt out) is positive, they bet heavier, as the odds favor them.

You can do the same thing in fantasy football in valuing possible positive or negative factors for your players. A team with a strong running game would give that RB a +1, an average running game would be -0- and a poor running attack would generate a -1. Now let's see who he is matched up against in the coming weeks. If the defense the RB is going against is tough, that generates a -1, average D would be a -0- and a poor D would be a +1. Therefore, a strong RB (+1) and a poor D (+1) would equal an overall score of 2. If that RB has many positive scores for the remaining weeks, you should try to trade for him. Of course, if the RB is showing some negatives for future games, trade him away. Always look at the projected scores during the playoff/championship weeks. This is not an absolute, but a general tendency. Most of the assistant coaches will already do the heavy lifting for you, just check out their updated info frequently.

"Rack'em and Stack'em" RB Mentality

You learned from the previous chapter to stack your roster with as many as six RBs (out of a roster of 14), but that doesn't mean you get to keep them. They were never meant to be hoarded, only for you to cherry pick. If you kept them all, over the long and hard season, this is what might happen:

There will be injuries in the NFL, most often hitting the RB position the hardest, so the coach that has the most RBs will be the most vulnerable. Why? If a coach had 6 RBs during the season, two of them will probably become injured, two more will turn out to be poor performers and the last two will be solid players for your team. The problem is you don't know which two will do what. Take your best educated guess and choose the best potential RBs to keep and look at trading the others. Your RBs (because of your 'bility) will become, as the season progresses, the strongest position on your team with the most depth. Always trade from your strength.

**The #1 rule in trading is to trade from your strength,
which can dictate better terms.**

Lucky You

Sometimes you will find one of your teams that, without you even trying, ends up having two stud position players – at the same position! Let's say you draft your QBs late and pick two. They both end up scoring strong points for your team and neither shows signs of slowing down. In keeping with the #1 rule above, trade one QB to help clean up your warts at another position on your team. Keeping both (with one on the bench) gives you zero points and is a waste of space. Each week you will have a tough decision. At times, you will pick the wrong one and beat yourself up. That takes the fun out of it. Trade from your strength. If you have no warts then, by all means, keep them both.

Apples and Oranges

Try to vary your trades; do not always look to trade a RB for a RB. It's much more advantageous to swap a QB for a RB or the many other possibilities. It's also easier to frame your value proposition to the other coach when your player can't be directly compared to your opposition's player who is in the same position.

The # 2 rule in trading is to trade apples for oranges.

7.4 - WHO WILL YOU BE TRADING WITH?

You will be playing against two types of coaches in your league, the experienced coach and the inexperienced coach. It will be very hard to find an advantage against an experienced coach. Your best plan of action is to identify and trade with an inexperienced coach.

WARNING: Please keep your status and strategies in mind and do not go hunting for the inexperienced coach just to make shortsighted trades. It may be exciting, but you still need your focus 100 percent of the time on the championship game.

The #3 rule in trading is to trade with the inexperienced coach.

Let's look at what some inexperienced coaches are like:

The Happy Trader

At the beginning of the season, you will always find a coach who just wants to trade for the sake of trading. He will state to all the other coaches that all of his players are available. It is important to note here that this coach had no strategy at all in the war room. In the early weeks, the value he puts on his players will be too high but, as the season wears on, he may very well be singing a different tune. If the season is not kind to him, his enthusiasm will be down, as well as his players' values. This is a perfect time to look at his roster and make him a happy trading partner. Keep your notes on who is a happy trader in your league.

The Homerism

If you did your "home"work in the war room, you now know where the other coaches' home-based locations are. Most coaches love having a player from their home NFL team playing for them. It's more exciting to talk about at the water cooler. They can't help themselves. If you want to trade a particular player, first find out where you could send him "home." That coach may be just too eager to accommodate you.

The Weak-Kneed Coach

Over the long grinding NFL season, most players will play better or worse than their original projections. Not all, but the majority will. When a good player hits a rough patch and lowers his points scored, an inexperienced coach will give up on him and lower his value. Trade for him now, while his value is low. On the other hand, you may have a poor player who has had two very hot weeks. Trade him off immediately, while his value is high. The "Weak-Kneed Coach" has the "what are you doing for me now?" mentality and doesn't plan for the projected future potential of a player. This inexperienced coach will also be vulnerable if one of his players is hobbling around. He won't have the patience to sit through the injury, and you can rightly assume he would like to move the "damaged" goods. If he wants to move a player with a lower value, you may just want to oblige.

7.5 - OTHER TRADING CONSIDERATIONS

The Byes Have It

As I've stated before, your opposition dreads having to deal with the NFL bye weeks, but you should love it. If you can trade for a player who has already been on a bye for your player with a bye week yet to come, that would be awesome.

Watch for the effects the bye weeks will have on the other teams. If you can pick up a player from your preferred player list and make another coach stronger for that week, he will love you for it. If a particular coach is in a "must-win" situation and staring at his bye week player, maybe he will be forced to make a trade. You could deal from your strength and bail him out in the short-term, helping yourself out long-term. Coming up to weeks 6 and 7 with six teams on byes each week may make for easy pickings.

An easy trade is helping a coach that needs a win and has a bye coming up.

After reading your leagues rules, you could possibly offer a trade with a bye week approaching which might get approved by the other coaches but not consummated by the Sunday deadline. When the consummation takes place after Wednesday, you get the player with his bye week safely in the past. If the other coach does not keep up on the rules, he can't hold you accountable.

The "bye" weeks have trade advantages written all over it. If you like, make sure you specialize in "bye week trading."

Lookie Lookie

Look at the other coaches' teams on a consistent basis. Find out where their warts are. Then, find a trade that makes them look good. They won't be able to resist. If your league site can break down individual position stats, you can easily see (as compared to every other coach in the league) where they are weak. Maybe it is his WR spot, or his defense. If you have strength (with proper depth) where his weakness is, it might be a match made in heaven.

Whenever an NFL injury happens, find the team that has the injured player to see if the coach needs a void filled. Look at their record, as a losing record indicates a desperate coach. Convince them not to give up playing the game and trade with you.

Division Rivals

The NFL teams will not trade in their own division during the season, as they can't afford to make a team they play twice a year any stronger than they already are. You need to keep the same thought process. Be very careful when you consider a trade with your direct competition. That is why I prefer smaller divisions of four teams instead of six teams. If you feel you have made the playoffs then, by all means, go ahead and make the advantageous trade.

If a division rival is ahead of your team for the playoffs, you might want to trade within your division to make another team strong enough to challenge the leader. Toward the end of the season, you will all be playing each other; therefore, try to trade with this "other" team after you have played him, but before the leader has played him. This is taking a calculated risk, but do the math toward the end of the season to see if it could work out.

Neat trading tip: Take the players away from your divisional rival that are on your preferred list that could hurt you at playoff time.

Trading rule #4 - Be very careful about making your division rivals stronger. It can come back to haunt you.

The Chatterbox

This may sound easy, but it is very time consuming if done correctly. This process must be kept up the entire year and you will need copious notes if you want to fully take advantage of the situation. However, if you are a natural social butterfly, you might actually have fun.

Always look to get a conversation going with the other coaches, even before any trading possibilities open up. Every time another coach speaks, he lets you know where he stands on certain issues. Every time you know where he stands, he makes himself weaker.

In the conversation, you should always talk up your players and their future potential. Do the hype and spin the good points of your players' performances. When talking about their players, tone down the "speak" and talk to the negative aspects of their players. Perhaps state that the defenses will stack the box against them or they are not getting to the red zone enough. The other coaches believe you are just talking but, in reality, you are setting up the future.

You must keep very good notes on all conversations. Do not stop talking after the trade has gone through, or they will catch on to your ruse. You will need to be a spin master all year long. For the actual trade offer, it would be best to talk to a person live or, if not live, try the phone. You are able to connect much easier if it's up close and personal. Always be ready to explain the win-win situation and reassure him there is no harm to any team.

WARNING! All of the information is this book is based on a standard league roster and performance scoring. If you play in a non-standard league, it is your responsibility to understand how any or all of the strategies can impact your team.

SportsLine is a registered service mark of SportsLine.com, Inc. All other brand names mentioned in this book are trade- or service marks of their respective companies.

THE LITTLE THINGS COUNT:
Compound Your Knowledge to Dominate

WHAT WILL BE REVIEWED:

1. The most important factors to remember
2. Learn from practical experiences

Overview

You have just read six revolutionary (sometimes complex) chapters about how to dominate fantasy football. Some of the subjects in this chapter have been covered in those chapters, but I now want to emphasize and expand upon some of the most important points to ensure they are retained by all readers.

The advice in this chapter may come in smaller pieces, but please don't discount it as unimportant based on its size. Every bit of knowledge you gain and implement will be compounded during the season. And you'll find that this chapter compounds all of the advice you've learned so far.

8.1 - KICK-O-RAMA

Though the kicker, as the last player drafted, doesn't get much respect, I haven't forgotten him. For the most part, all kickers start out fairly identical, but some do have advantages over others.

Let's play with the kicker position.

Dropkick Version 1

If you draft very early in the preseason, as soon as the draft is over, you'll want to drop the kicker you were forced to take by the rules. This will give you an extra roster spot to play around with during the preseason. When the NFL season begins, you can go out and pickup a good kicker from the free agent pool.

Dropkick Version 2

Because there are plenty of good kickers all season long, when the bye week rolls around, most coaches, who have fewer open roster spots available, will drop their kickers and pick up replacements from the player pool with the intention of picking their original kickers back up the following week. This is done all the time. Knowing this tendency can give you a real plus in filling out your roster with the preferred kicker you were unable to draft.

Watch this! The kicker you truly covet (for the championship game) is on a bye in Week 8. Earlier in the season, you pick a solid kicker who has a bye in Week 9. You play your solid kicker all year long. Your opposition will drop his kicker in Week 8 (unless he is on fire). In Week 9, you drop your

Ahhh, the life of a kicker.

kicker and pick up your coveted kicker. Keep in mind *if* he has an earlier waiver pick than you on Week 9, you need to grab him as a free agent in Week 8 on Sunday. Most likely only you and the coach that dropped him will be interested in using a waiver position for a kicker. Brilliant!!

Why didn't you just pick this coveted kicker up at the draft? Because then you would have had to drop your kicker (during preseason) and hope you get him back, or be forced to carry two kickers at some point. You never want to take up two roster spots for kickers.

WARNING! Coaches are reluctant to drop big-name kickers; therefore, if you want a successful dropkick, don't covet the big-name kicker.

8.2 - THE 50 PERCENT RULE

I talked before about the luck factor being part of the 50 percent rule. The 50 percent rule is here to help you understand that you can't control things which you do not have control of in the first place. Therefore, spend time on only the items that you *can* control. This rule actually has three different meanings.

1. At any given time, with no advantage, you'll win one-half of your games and lose one-half of your games. It is pretty much a coin flip. You'll increase your odds only when you find strategies to give you advantages.

2. During the season, you'll have some gut wrenching choices between two players and you can only choose one. You can break down your decisions in many ways to try to help you make the final choice but, at the end of the season, if you kept a diary, you would find your hard choices were 50 percent correct and 50 percent incorrect. Learn to live with this and try not to be disappointed.

3. When drafting your team, you will be lucky if 50 percent of the top-tier projected players end up as top-tier players by the end of the year. This is the meat and potatoes of the 50 percent rule. There are no sure things; therefore, you don't need to sweat about any particular player. Let your strategy dictate your draft.

> **That super stud you draft in the first round truly has only a 50 percent chance of returning to the top. Focus instead on your overall team concept.**

8.3 - WHAT HAPPENS IF YOU LOSE YOUR FIRST-ROUND STUD?

For many fantasy football coaches, losing their first-round stud is a panic situation. After all, they have built him up to be the foundation of their team, and have dreams of him scoring bountiful points all year long. Readers of this book, however, know that injuries or other factors are the facts of the game and that you must live with the fickle finger of fate. With that said:

> **The team concept will always champion over a stud.**

Yes, your job would be *easier* if you had an RB stud on your team but, as long as you have the team concept, you can overcome losing your very first pick. Much will depend on *when* you lose your stud. If you lose him in the beginning of the season, you have the rest of the year to fill the roster spot. Many opportunities will appear, although the quality may not be quite as good.

How my stud went down early:

I had drafted Deuce McAllister as my first-round stud on four of my 21 teams before Hurricane Katrina hit in 2005. (After Katrina, I did not draft him again, as I quickly realized all his games would be "away" games.) He went down in the middle of Week 5 and was lost for the season. Of those four teams, I made the playoffs with three. And, of those three, I won the championship with one. Even without a sure first-round choice, you can make it to the playoffs. Once you get into the playoff games, anything can happen.

Because you have the 'bility on your side, you will stack your team with running backs throughout the year. You may have to call on them in the beginning or at the end but, as long as you raid the player pool, you will have options.

How my stud went down at the end of the season:

In 2005, I had D. Davis on six of my teams in the beginning of the NFL season. He was a consensus first-round pick in most drafts. In our first-round playoff game in Week 15 of the NFL season, with 30 minutes before the Sunday kickoff, the coach announced Davis would not be starting (didn't warm up well). Therefore, almost one-third of my teams (six out of 21) lost their stud RB with mere moments before the players were locked. I made my switches (with mild panic) and all six of those teams went on to victory without Mr. Davis.

For the championship game the following week, Mr. Davis was off again and it was also decided on Friday of that week that the Indianapolis Colts wouldn't play their starters the full game. I had E. James as my first-round stud on seven teams. Very loud OUCH. So there I was in the championship round with 13 total first-round studs out of 21 teams (62 percent) riding the pine. To add insult to injury, I had my "stacked" wide receivers of Marvin Harrison or Reggie Wayne filling 18 of the available roster spots for wide receivers (42 total spots available) because Indianapolis wouldn't play all their studs. That was another 43 percent of my wide receivers who wouldn't be playing to their maximum potential, if at all. Things were not looking very bright, but I ended up winning 85 percent of my championship games. If I can win with everything going wrong at the very last minute, I think anybody can do it. You have to be prepared for the worst and be ready to dominate the championship game. If those players had played for me, there is no doubt in my mind I would have won 100 percent of both my first-round playoff games and my championship games.

Can you overcome the odds when you lose your first round stud? Absolutely. It just makes your job a little bit harder.

What if you lose your first two picks? What do you think I am, a magician? We do have to be realists, don't we?

8.4 - FANTASY FOOTBALL POINTS VS. THE NFL

Every week, all 12 fantasy football teams score points and win or lose their game. It's the same situation in the NFL, but realize that the NFL games will score fewer points and the margin of victory will be much smaller than for the fantasy football teams. You need to understand this difference and don't get caught up in the NFL scoring format while playing fantasy football. Many inexperienced coaches make their decisions based on the scoring format of successful NFL teams. These teams affect fantasy football only indirectly. The average win margin is by 24.3 points in my leagues. Most NFL teams do not even score that many points on a weekly basis.

8.5 - WHEN TO USE A PLAYER ON A BYE WEEK

The bye week forces you to make decisions about your starting lineup. Most coaches have never considered purposely starting a player who will give you a guaranteed "0" for that position. However, there may come a time, although rarely, when it's in your team's best interest to use this strategy.

To use this strategy, you must incorporate three or four items to keep your eyes planted firmly on the championship:

1. Is your "bility maxed out?
2. Is the team you are playing very weak?
3. What is your team's record at this point?
4. Who is available on the waiver?

Remember, as long as your strategy was to have the late season byes, then you can readily see how your team's direction is going. Let's say your 'bility is indeed maxed out and you have no one player you wish to drop without hurting your team in the long run. Your opponent for this particular week appears beatable and you also have a strong win-loss record like 6-2. This could be the perfect situation to suck it up and take a zero.

We all have those games which we win by 1, 2, 3, or 4 points or lose by that same number. With the former, we are elated, as it will count as a win just as much as a victory by 30 points. With the latter, we are dejected and looking at the "what if." The truth is most games are decided by an average of 24.3 points; therefore, in many cases, a player scoring a few points will not impact your record. See stats in section 10.2.

There are only three positions which you should consider taking a goose egg for points – kicker, tight end and, in some cases, defense. These positions can very easily score only three or four points in any given week. This will not make or break your team. As an example, say you have Antonio Gates and his team is on a bye. Your opponent has a tight end that averages four points a game. You can rest assured with your decision to "start" Antonio Gates instead of trying to find another very marginal tight end in the player pool. You'll probably find that you still win 50 percent of your games playing a player short.

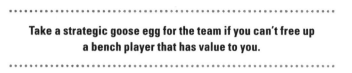

Take a strategic goose egg for the team if you can't free up a bench player that has value to you.

The NFL bye weeks are Weeks 3 through 9 and, as previously discussed, you should bunch your star player's byes not only in the same week but in the latter part of the season. By the time Week 9 rolls around, your bye problem may have solved itself in your waiver wire and free agent pick ups.

In 2005, I started some "non-starters" and those bye week blues were actually some of my highest scoring games of the year.

8.6 - WHEN TO THROW A GAME

In the NFL, toward the end of the season, many teams for many different reasons will bench their stars. What they're essentially saying is they're not planning to win. You may have your own reasons to bench your starters and say you're not planning to win. I don't advocate that you do anything illegal or immoral. However, just as in the NFL, you are here to win the championship and you must use everything at your disposal to get to that level.

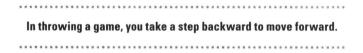

In throwing a game, you take a step backward to move forward.

The opportunity to throw a game doesn't come very often but, when it does, you need to be ready to act. Remember, no one will win every game and knowing that can make it easier to choose "when" you should lose.

Your first opportunity to throw a game may come at the beginning of the fantasy football season. In most fantasy football leagues, the rules state that whoever finishes last in their league will receive the first waiver pick for the following week. In the first few weeks of the NFL season, you may be able to see gems starting to form on the waiver wire. And, of course, there is the "all present" injury. With those factors in mind, losing one of the first three games is not all bad, as you could have the possibility of a good pick up. A nice pick up would be defined as one that would make a stronger team as the season progresses. Possibly you'll find you have already lost the game early on (being blown out). At that time, move your starters in your late games to the bench, thus lowering your point total and helping you get a better waiver pick on tiebreakers.

Sometimes you can just lower your points scored for the week and end up with the same results. Therefore, in the middle of the Sunday games (early in the season), review the current situation.

In 2005, I did this on one of my teams in the very first week to grab Willie Parker of Pittsburgh. I didn't throw the game, as I was already losing, but there were five other losers to compete with. I lowered my points by benching some players, which ensured that I got the first waiver pick, and guaranteed that Mr. Parker was going to play for me. How did I know if he was going to perform well? I didn't, but he was having one fine game that Sunday and was very much worth the risk. You must take bold steps to win.

The second opportunity to throw a game, or at least not play your strongest team, comes with the NFL bye weeks. My strategy is to bunch as many of my stars on the same bye week. When that particular week comes, if I don't feel I can fill the roster spots, I just take a loss and live with it. On the weeks my team has no byes, I will field my strongest team and will adjust to the loss the bye selection gave me – if that's what it comes down to. Of course, having the late byes won't necessitate this move.

The third opportunity to drop a game or lower your points is the final week before the playoffs. If you have already made the playoffs, you may want to try to play match up to determine which coach you will oppose in the playoffs. Of course, your preference would be to play the weakest team (which I hope is not you). If you read your rules to see how the play-offs will match up, you may find that, in losing a game, you get a much easier match. You probably will not know for sure which opponent you will have, as they may have to win or lose their game, but you can take a calculated guess. I would much rather go up against a coach that has 11 wins but just lost his star running back last week, then go up against one that has nine wins but his running back will be playing next week against a very soft defense. Most of the time, your game will not impact who you will play, but study the situation and plan accordingly.

**If possible, control your destiny and choose your playoff
opponent by sacking a game.**

Some league commissioners won't look at this tactic very fondly, as they believe that life itself should always be fair. To be fair to everybody, they believe, we should always play our very best game and our very best players every week. What happens in one week or another is not a concern to me – I only care about what happens in the championship game. I play to win. If I were to throw a game and it would impact one or more of my competitors who just happen to be right on the bubble, too bad. It's not my fault he or she is on the bubble. Can two other teams collude against me if the timing is right? Sure, but if I have to depend on them, then maybe I won't go very far anyway.

You absolutely do **not** throw a game to help a friend or relative make the playoffs. That would be immoral and illegal. If you have the power to help a competitor make the playoffs and it clears the way for your own championship run, recognize that you will have to decide to use that power on by a case-by-case basis and still be able to look in the mirror. Remember, if you put a competitor in the playoffs, your actions are eliminating somebody else, which may not be considered fair. However, you are to play the best game possible in order for you to reach the championship round. That may entail actually throwing a game.

8.7 - REACHING FOR A PLAYER

Coaches tend to believe too much in the published draft position and projections. History has taught us to use common sense and football IQ together and, if you must reach for a player to anchor your team concept, don't hesitate. That doesn't mean you reach for every player in the draft. Every game invented has risk but, along with the risks, come rewards.

8.8 - YOU CAN'T HAVE TOO MANY RBS

You have a ton of strategies to work with, but, the bottom line throughout the whole season is to load up on the RB wagon train. After the draft, the RB position gives you the greatest potential. Look to your own team's needs first and then automatically focus on the RB. You must grab the RBs before your opponents even start to consider a particular player. Many of your RB choices won't work out and be dropped accordingly but, the more pieces of coal you put in your stocking, the more diamonds you may find forming.

8.9 - HANDCUFFS

There is nothing like having your main man go down with an injury and you have no player to replace him. The easiest method of replacement is to have his backup on your roster. You need to handcuff your studs in order to guarantee this roster position for your team. The more you handcuff, the less 'bility you have. When you do this is up to you. If your comfort level goes way up by grabbing your handcuff early, then so be it. Or you can watch your league tendencies to see when handcuffs start disappearing from the waiver wire. Usually when the waiver wire runs thin on good choices, the handcuffs start to look more appealing. In my experience, this is about Week 10 of the NFL season; therefore, I beat the rush and get my chosen handcuffs around Week 8 or 9. Yes, this is a bit riskier, but my strategy is to maximize my 'bility as long as I reasonably can.

> In 2004, I was totally taken by surprise by the other smart coaches when I lost my handcuffs at Week 10. In 2005, I made sure I didn't get caught with my pants down.

On some teams, the clear handcuff is anything but clear. Picking the wrong handcuff could put your handcuff strategy in jeopardy. What do you do then? Easy – stay away from that particular starter the whole season. Do not put yourself in the position of not knowing. There are too many variables as it is. Let your opponent have that worry.

The handcuff can also work for other positions. The QB is an obvious choice, especially if you have a heavy passing team with an easy schedule. The WR could be unique. If you find two good WRs on one team (which translates into heavy passing numbers) and one goes down, the #3 moves up into this slot. If you re-read the above sentence it states that you have a handcuff that could fill either (two) position. That is almost a two-fer.

In 2005, in many weeks on many teams, when I had my 'bility working but didn't have any quality long-term players to pick up, I went and grabbed a #3 WR on a strong team for a week. You never know what will happen and he makes an excellent spotter.

8.10 - DEFENSES ON THE WAIVER WIRE

If defenses are not important to your league in scoring points, you may want to skip this paragraph. At CBS SportsLine, the defense does play an important part. It's very hard to pick a top-line defense from the previous year's numbers. After the draft, you may not know until after the first three or four weeks if your defense is playing as strong as they need to be. The first three or four weeks of the NFL season will give you ample time to audition another defense that is still on the waiver wire. They may just end up surprising everyone (even the experts) by year's end. I have preached to keep only one kicker, one tight end and one defense throughout the season to give you the most 'bility; however, watch for a defense in the early season and maybe take a flier. If both defenses remain strong, strongly consider keeping the best and trading the remaining D to give you back your maximum 'bility throughout the season.

8.11 - SERIOUS ABOUT THE TEAM

You are playing the match up in the championship game when you do your draft. Every coach loves to play match up games if they have the ability to work the proper angles (most will not have this ability). Most coaches will look at match ups when they're serious about their teams and they usually get serious too late in the season.

You'll also find that the other coaches will look at match ups at different times of the season. It all depends on when they "catch on." The longer it takes before they catch on to the match up, the better for you.

> *In my league, I found that after Week 10, most fantasy football coaches were starting to look at the match up possibilities for their team. That's way too late.*

Most coaches don't look ahead. The exception would be in their upcoming bye week. Truly, all they are looking for is how to win the upcoming game. They are not even trying to improve their team, as no one has yet shared this secret. You, on the other hand, are always thinking ahead.

8.12 - PLANNING A WEEK AHEAD

It's amazing to me that the average population does not plan ahead in any endeavor. In fact, planning should be the cornerstone of any undertaking or, should I say, any *successful* undertaking. Planning ahead will put you many steps in front of your competition in anything you do – including fantasy football.

After every week's game, the first thing you need to do is look ahead two or three weeks to look for any weaknesses in your personal schedule. Be aware that, by the time that week is here, things may have changed. Therefore, not everything you do will work out and flexibility again becomes one of your best friends.

If you fail to plan, you plan to fail.
Planning ahead is paramount to your success.

After looking at your personal schedule for your teams, you can check out your opposition's roster for the next couple of weeks. Possibly there is something you can pick up to upset his applecart.

Even if there are no good choices on the waiver wire, you can look at the match ups with marginal players, if you have the space for the week.

I have picked up many marginal players on Saturday or Sunday with the hopes that they kick start their season that week and, if it turns out that they didn't, I would drop them like lead balloons on Tuesday and move on. It didn't harm my team and had the potential to help it. My 'bility gave me this throughout the season.

8.13 - PLAYING THREE GAMES IN ONE

When the average coach plays, they are only thinking of playing one game at a time. You, however, are actually playing three games at a time.

1. Your first game is setting yourself up for the championship run.

2. Your second game is looking ahead to the next two to six weeks through the upcoming schedule and making your plans.

3. Your third game is playing the "one game" at a time.

This makes your job more complex, especially since you are not dealing just with your team but 11 other teams and the NFL schedule. Most other coaches will not put the time in that is necessary to dominate. Set yourself up to out work, out hustle, and outsmart your opposition.

8.14 - DRAFT WITHIN A DRAFT

During the draft, the average coach is one-dimensional, while you are doing a draft within draft. Their one-dimensional draft is just getting the players that they favor for their team.

Your draft consists of:
1. The dual purpose draft for:
    a. The current competitive team
    b. The championship run

2. Watching your competition:
    a. Your competition could be the teams in your division.
    b. A competitor that you've seen draft before and know his tendencies.
    c. If you're at either ends of the draft, your competition could be working the corner teams.

8.15 - STRENGTH OF SCHEDULE (SOS)

The strength of schedule goes hand-in-hand with playing match ups for the future. You need to review this often as the strength of schedule changes with each NFL game. My suggestion is to examine the strength of schedule every three to four weeks through one of your assistant coaches. When you view the SOS, break down the future in four-week segments. Each segment will have different winners and losers and you can use this review to see if there's anything that could help your team. However, as stated, concentrate on the championship and playoff rounds, always watching for changes for the end of the season.

Break down the SOS into four week segments and review the changes every few weeks.

8.16 - THURSDAY NIGHT GAMES

In most leagues, the Thursday night games will lock the player pool for the entire NFL and fantasy football leagues regardless if your team is playing on Thursday. In 2006, the NFL will play many more Thursday night games. In most leagues, this will be a detriment to your teams, for the simple reason that you need the week to play out your advantages. Therefore, you lose some advantage over your opposition. This will be new to everyone, however, different advantages can be found. You just need to look.

The Thursday night game will limit every coach's strategy but that doesn't mean you can't find advantages within the system. I can guarantee that most of the other coaches will look at the limits put on them and just shrug their shoulders; your job is to work out the solutions.

I will be working very hard to review this schedule change and the impact on my team. You should, too.

Changes mean finding new solutions.

8.17 - THE BYE TRADER

Yes, I know we had a chapter on trading and I told you to not spend a great deal of time on this. It's not the trading you should focus on, but how the other coaches mismanage and fear the bye week. The trading desk gives an avenue to the bye week coaches.

If you feel you can improve your team through the trade process, then you really do want to specialize with the byes. The bye week should be one of the most important advantages in playing fantasy football. Most coaches have not even considered this, as they just plain hate the bye weeks and what it forces them to do. If you have an unhappy coach, you may possibly have a happy trading partner.

In 2006, almost 20 percent of the NFL teams will be off Week 6 and Week 7. This is new and a golden opportunity for you. Let's say that it's Week 5 and your opponent has just realized he has three players off on Week 7 and is in panic mode. You, however, always had an eye on this certain RB (of his) that you didn't draft on purpose, hoping you could get him as a trade if he proved he could produce. If you offered another capable RB to get this RB during the bye week, he may be forced to jump, especially if he needs the victory to stay in the fantasy hunt.

Trading is only an avenue to use for the bye week grab bag.

After the draft, look for those strong players you covet in weeks 6 and 7 and watch other teams' progress to see if a trade is possible down the road. Make your notes at the draft, bring them out in Week 5 and look strongly at some trade proposals. I assure you there will be some teams caught flatfooted, as this is the first time the NFL has done this.

8.18 - THE END GAME – GO FOR THE THROAT

If you've made it this far to the playoffs, congratulations. But your job isn't over; your job is to win it all. We are to assume you have a pretty solid team, one that is capable of scoring a hundred points plus. If it isn't, you have to search the waiver wire to fill your holes. However, if you planned ahead, you shouldn't have any huge holes to fill. Now you're ready to crush your opponent, don't let him breathe, – step on him and step hard.

All your work is for naught if you can't go for the kill. You've built up your team to its highest potential and are now free to put up any road-blocks against your opposition.

Teacher say, kick butt.

For the championship game, your team needs to be set up differently. You are playing against one team only and aren't concerned about the future. You want to look for advantages but not the same ones as during the season. Now is the time to bring it home. Dominate, dominate, dominate.

> *I had a friend who played in the CBS leagues with more teams than even I bought – 30. With 30 teams, I would think one could draw the conclusion that a person is very serious about winning. He made the championship game in 12 of his leagues, which is OK.* **He won exactly six championships.** *Six of 12 is basically a coin flip. Alas, he was not prepared to dominate.*

> *In early 2005, there was a book published called* Win at Fantasy Football. *The authors of this book had a web site and they published the end results for their 2005 teams. Of their 13 teams, they made the playoffs in 10. That in itself is very impressive.* **They brought home the championship, however, in one league only.** *Again, they were not prepared for the championship game. It's not how many games you win but is what you do on that special week.*

To set up your team for the championship game, you need a different mindset. Since you play only eight players and you are down to the last couple of weeks, you need to stack your roster **with stability** as your main driver. Since you no longer have to look several weeks ahead, you won't need the 'bility to funnel future gems. That will allow you to have about three roster spots available.

Now, you want to find your opponent's warts and exploit them. You want to try to do this at least a week ahead, as proper planning would have you do. If you don't know who your opponent will be that following week, it pays to take your best guess and plan accordingly. You probably have a 50 percent chance of being correct.

Your bench roster will be entirely different during the season as compared to the playoffs and especially the championship game.

If your opponent is very smart, he probably won't have any warts to attack. Luckily for you, most of your opposition won't be the brightest and will not only have warts, but large ones. Most of your opposition will be limping into the championship game.

During this part of the NFL season, there will be many RBs coming on the scene due to injuries. It may behoove you to snatch up any and all just to keep them off of your opponent's team. He may even be very solid at the RB position, at least at the moment, but then the news hits the airwaves and one of his RBs moves from probable to doubtful. As he is sitting on his hands, thinking the news may improve, you have heard enough and will click that mouse to pick up that particular backup. Don't let him breathe.

Check out the NFL schedule and determine if your opponent's defense will have a hard time scoring points at the championship game. If you believe it will, great! Make sure there are no alternatives in defenses out there for him to pick.

Don't forget to look at your competition's kicker. Is he kicking in a dome or possibly in bad weather?

Do you see my point? You'll take care of your own team first, but look at your opposition's upcoming situation and be a week or two ahead of him.

At this stage of the game, injuries are your friends. They can't take *you* down, but your opponent will be vulnerable.

*In 2005, I had one opponent drop his kicker on Tuesday before the championship game, as he wanted to pick up another player and evaluate. At the time, there were 18 other kickers on the waiver wire and he felt very comfortable that I couldn't put all 18 on my roster. I saw this huge wart starting to fester on Tuesday and kept quiet until Saturday morning (one minute after midnight). Systematically, I went and picked up every kicker and then dropped every kicker, one by one. That locked up every kicker until Sunday. On Sunday at 12 noon, **all** players in the player pool were locked. Was my opponent upset? You bet. He was a huge favorite to win this championship game, but going without a kicker sure wouldn't help his cause. As it turns out, I won the championship easily and didn't need this tactic. If your opposition plays dumb, you just play smart. Again, some league commissioners may try to say this was misusing the waiver system, but I would argue that I used their rules and I only play one way – to win.*

The strategies got you this far, but now you must look at your team in a different light. Everyone on your roster has a purpose and it's definitely short-term. Should you handcuff your opponent's RB? Probably not during the regular season, as this would be a poor use of your 'bility. However, during the playoffs and especially with the championship game on the horizon, it could be an excellent hedge. If your opponent has not protected his own roster in this way, he is living dangerously and deserves any punishment you can deliver.

8.19 - CHAMPIONSHIP GAME TIEBREAKER

It's Sunday morning of the championship round. Your lineup is set and ready to dominate. I have neglected to tell you one more point. There's a remote chance you will have a tie at the end of the day. Every league has tiebreakers. Read your league's rules to find out what that tie-breaker is for the championship round. Ten minutes before kickoff, maximize your tie-breaker advantage. Don't tip your hand too early, as the other coach may figure it out and play your same game. Ties are rare, but you have come this far, so follow through.

> *In 2004, my opponent maximized his tie-breaking advantage. I didn't have a clue and was, in fact, sitting at my computer just laughing. Color me red, as we did indeed tie and he won the tiebreaker handily. It cost me over $3,000. In 2005, I did my own maximization and was ready; however, there were no ties for my games.*

8.20 - DIARY

Most coaches will find many things they like about this book and will implement some strategies or ideas. However, I know most of you will dismiss keeping a diary. Yes, it may make sense, but is just too much work. Keeping a diary or logbook for each league will have very low impact for this year. However, a thorough diary can increase your odds for the future. That is, if you learn from your, and the other coaches', mistakes. In everything we do on this earth (and fantasy football is no different), history has a way of repeating itself. The history will tell you exactly how to play the game. In any sport, you'll find the great ones understand how the game is played, but they play it under their terms.

8.21 - PRACTICE

If you want to be the best at anything in life, you must practice. It can't be overstated that you must practice the draft. I have found the Draft

Dominator to be ideal to hone your skills. Although the draft is not the most important part of your fantasy football season, it is a very significant piece of your championship run. You always want to get started out in front of the pack. If you are prepared, there will be no surprises. Remember, as we discussed in a previous chapter, your draft has to be dual-purpose. This makes your job more complex than your opposition's, who is just trying to find their favorite players.

8.22 - PLAYING FAVORITES

The average coach has his coveted players and, by golly, he will do what it takes to get them. To choose your favorite player is most likely your emotion at work. A disciplined plan has no room for emotion. Choose a player or players for what he brings to your team. Use your emotion to choose your favorite foods.

8.23 - CLEAN UP YOUR WARTS

There is no fantasy football team that will start the season out as the favorite and end up as the winner, unless they improve their team during the season. Every team will have warts at the beginning of the season. It's your responsibility to clean up those warts and the waiver wire is the best tool to do this. You'll want a 50 percent annual turnover for your team from the beginning of the season to the end. You can get by with a little bit more or less than 50 percent, but keep it fairly close. Does that mean you only drop six or seven players during the year? Not at all, you may end up having 30 or 40 total pick ups to find those five or six players that improve your team. Be active on the waiver wire, but play smart.

8.24 - KEEP YOUR GOAL IN SIGHT

There are so many ways to get off track during the season if you don't focus all your energies and steps towards the championship game. Every once in awhile, you'll have to take a step that will help you short-term, but you need to make sure that it is the exception to the rule. With every step, ask yourself, "Will this move help or hurt my team for my ultimate goal, the championship game?" Knowing you will not win every game, or for that matter every league, helps keep the pressure off during the season. If these strategies are played correctly, you'll find yourself in the middle of the season grinding out wins and wondering if you're on the right path. To be able to dominate the championship game, you have to sacrifice during the season. Don't get off track.

8.25 - NO THIRD-RATE PLAYERS

Every roster spot on your team should have a reason for being there. It should be individualized for your particular team to fill its needs, wants, and, most importantly, to clean up your warts. You should never have a player on your team for the sole reason to sit and look pretty; make sure every player has his purpose. If their purpose is no longer needed, drop them immediately. The purpose could be for short-term or long-term, but make sure they are pulling their weight.

I am continually amazed at my opposition coaches who choose to have wide receivers, tight ends, and running backs who, although they are playing a full NFL game, are never going to play for a fantasy football team because their average points scored is in the three to four point range. That will not win you championships. But I see them on the rosters of my opposition week in and week out.

8.26 - DON'T GET TOO CUTE

It's very easy in fantasy football to out think yourself. The best advice I can give you concerning this is to have more than one assistant coach and compare their advice. If both of them or all (if more than 2) are saying the exact same thing or very similar, do not question, just follow. Sometimes the more you think about a situation the more you'll shoot yourself in the foot. You'll find yourself in less than a 50/50 proposition. You hired your assistant coaches for reasons. Follow them.

8.27 - SIT ON YOUR HANDS

In chess, we learn when you see a good move, sit on your hands and look for a better move. It works. In fantasy football, sometimes you have to make quick decisions because of the ever-changing news blasted to you via your e-mail. There are times you should sit and wait before you pull the trigger. An example of this would be to do your Sunday lineup on Saturday and sleep on it. Sunday morning, you can review your choices to see if your thinking still holds true. Never do a full line up on the day of the game. Another example would be the waiver pick up. Do your waiver wire work on Tuesday, let it sit overnight and then review your ideas on Wednesday. Always challenge yourself and look for that better move.

8.28 - WEEK 17 IS FOR THE NFL ONLY

Before joining a fantasy football league, read their rules. Under the schedule, look for when the championship game is being played. Week 17 is not acceptable, although many leagues still do this. In Week 17, there are too many NFL teams "resting" their stars because they have their own playoff spot locked in. If your league uses Week 17, this could easily make for a very unfair advantage and is not an equitable way to crown a fantasy football champion. If your top players are sitting on the bench, all your hard work could be thrown down the toilet.

In 2005, Indianapolis Colts actually started "resting" their starters in Week 16. In 2004, it was the Philadelphia Eagles. Sometimes it happens in earlier weeks, but Week 17 is notorious for this action.

8.29 - HOW MANY TEAMS SHOULD YOU OWN?

Each person has to decide how many teams is the right fit for them. But in reading this book, I hope you figure out not all situations will come up for one team in any given year. Also know that any one team can be snake bit in scoring high but losing week after week after week. Injuries or busts to your studs can ruin the season as well. Therefore, if you want to have guaranteed fun, you need more than one team.

Before you decide the number of teams to take on, look at your research time. If you bought four advice web sites and spread that advice over three teams, think about how you could spread the exact same advice over six teams. It would be more economical in money and time.

Besides your normal research, go to the quickie web sites for the latest information three times a day – morning, your lunch break and late evenings. You must also be ready for the latest updates to come through your e-mail. Hopefully, you have the ability to act on those updates before your opponent.

Your quickie info should take about two hours per week. Your normal research should take about one hour per day, or seven hours per week. Decision-making for your teams runs about 15 minutes per team per week. As you can see, the teams are the least amount of time. Therefore, the more teams you want to have fun with (and dominate with) can extrapolate from your research time.

My advice is that between four and eight teams will use your full potential. The total of 26 teams (21 for CBS, three for ESPN and two others) that I did in 2005 controls too much of a person's time, but I did have fun!!!

8.30 - EQUIPMENT NEEDS

It sure is nice to have everything working smoothly. If you choose to go the extra mile to leverage your time and knowledge, consider what this equipment can do for you.

1. Spreadsheet software. Most of us know how to use a spreadsheet program like Microsoft Excel®. If you do not, you need to learn the basics so you can make worksheets that can fit your particular needs, not only in the pre-draft but also in the heat of the season. It will only serve to make your job easier and can be customized in any way your brain sees fit. Also, your information is portable. If you have to take a trip during the season, you need some information at your fingertips.

2. High-speed Internet access. You need information fast, especially if you are receiving advice from more than one location. There is nothing more frustrating than a slow old-fashioned dial-up connection.

3. Dual computer screens. This may seem a little bit unusual but, once you have tried it, you'll wonder how you could possibly get along without it. Besides helping you at fantasy football, it can be used in your everyday computer work.

Using one computer, you'll need to have two screens. Yes, your computer man can set up one hard drive and one mouse to work with two computer screens with different information on them at the same time.

You may want your Excel spreadsheets on one screen, as you're looking at an advice web site on the other screen. Maybe you're trying to set your starters for your league on one screen and looking at the weekly rankings on the other. Absolutely you could be doing your draft on one screen and have the Draft Dominator on the other screen (very handy). The two screens will leverage your strategies tremendously. Yes, you can always minimize and maximize with one screen but is not very efficient and, when you get frustrated, you tend to do less work.

All hobbies should be fun and, as they take up your time, some of them may require a monetary investment. If that investment makes your hobby more pleasurable (or efficient), it is well worth it. Have fun and enjoy!

WARNING! All of the information is this book is based on a standard league roster and performance scoring. If you play in a non-standard league, it is your responsibility to understand how any or all of the strategies can impact your team.

SportsLine is a registered service mark of SportsLine.com, Inc. All other brand names mentioned in this book are trade- or service marks of their respective companies.

CHAPTER 8 - THE LITTLE THINGS COUNT

CHAPTER 9

INFORMATION — BE BLOOD THIRSTY:
How to Get the Most out of Your Assistant Coaches

WHAT YOU WILL LEARN:

1. How to take advantage of the best resources
2. The tools that can make your season

Overview

Knowledge is power and the assistant coaches have the knowledge. If you want to be successful, you need to put the assistant coaches (advice web sites) on your team.

Geeks, super geeks, whatever you want to call them, these guys know their stats backwards and forwards. I personally can fill this book with strategies, but we need the geeks' statistics to work with our strategies. You or I do not have one-tenth of their knowledge when it comes to the statistics or, better yet, access to years of the past stats. I want these geeks on *my* side.

Every week, the geeks will give you more information than you can handle. They will tell you their opinions on who to start on Sunday, who to pick up on the waiver wire during the week and, if they are very good, they will help you look in the future to maximize your 'bility. You need them to help you form your gut opinions. You need them for ideas that you possibly never considered.

9.1 - ASSISTANT COACHES CAN HELP

There are hundreds of advice sites out there in the Internet land. Some are free and some are not; some are good and some are not. Your job is to get a stable of high-octane sites to advise you. If you only get your advice from your contest site, you are destined to lose. You need to have more than one source, as you can use each of them for confirmation of the other. Verification is important.

How many sites do you need? That is up to your time and money constraints. Just because you subscribe to a site, it doesn't mean you have to read every morsel they publish. Find things on each site you like and make it part of your overall plan. However, I would advise a maximum of four assistant coaches.

Groom your stable of assistant coaches annually. Every year, drop the site that you think performed the poorest, then go review five other sites as possibilities and choose one. By doing this, you are keeping the sites with which you're comfortable and expanding your portfolio of advice. It's very important to grow.

Toward the end of the season, many sites will "open" for free or at a lowered price. Check them out to prepare for the following year.

I require at least half of my assistant coaches to provide me with latest information instantly. This can make or break a team. If they get updated information about a player, I need that in my e-mail box. I don't want to have to go to their site to read it.

Your opposition usually subscribes to one site, which means he has limited his game.

I also prefer a site that is very good at giving me the latest information one hour before game time. Some are better at this than others, but this is a must, especially later in the NFL season.

Bonus Time

Wow, you're definitely playing fantasy football at the right time. The information available is not only getting better every year, but more and more sites are giving away extras with their already ridiculously low prices, and these extras are FREE. The business of running an advice web site must be getting more cutthroat – and we are the winners.

A few extras they are throwing in with subscriptions are:
1. Free tools to help our games
2. Free "easy" FF games, that sometimes pays huge $$$

Now that's what I call a very "friendly" assistant coach. It's a great value for your money!

Okay, here is what we are going to do.   *Yeah, here is what we are going to do.*

Be in the know before you park your dough.

Yes, there are hundreds of "assistant coaches" out there. I can't look at them all (I actually reviewed about 90 originally in 2005). On the next few pages I've listed over one hundred with comments on some of my favorites. You must determine for yourself if they deserve a spot on your team. After the assistant coaches, I have also listed some other sites for your pleasure.

Whichever site you choose to review, go to their link page and you will find a wealth of options. Happy hunting!

9.2 - ADVICE WEB SITES

FantasyFootballChamps.com
You can use this site for the advice, presented in a very unique way, with their FFCPI (the most powerful predictor tool available today) or you can upgrade and put these boys (Jon & Ian) as your personal co-coaches. They know what they're talking about when it comes to winning your league. When the pedal hits the metal, you want these guys on your side.
1. Customizable cheatsheet for **each** team
2. Track your teams from anywhere on the internet
3. Free FF game for cash

A must have purchase!

FootballGuys.com
Another one of my very favorite sites. You cannot out-read them as they produce over 30,000 pages of information a year. From so much data to choose from, you will find your favorite weekly information to help your team. Mine were the insights on the player stats after the week's games were played. That showed me the gems forming.

1. Many freebie tools including the Draft Dominator
2. Excellent free FF game

A no-brainer purchase!

TheHuddle.com

Since 1997, The Huddle has been the leading fantasy football information site on the Internet. In fact, The Huddle was voted the #1 Fantasy Football web site for five years in a row. It provides articles, analysis, rankings and cheatsheets for draft help each summer. During the season, you'll find player projections, game predictions, starting lineup advice, roster recommendations and breaking news to assist fantasy team owners in managing their team.

1. Love the "quick decision" weekly rankings
2. Free FF game

You cannot go wrong with this site!

FFMastermind.com

Fantasy Football Mastermind Inc. is a nationally recognized Internet-based information service leader that has been providing everything (both free & premium products) a fantasy football owner needs to dominate their league since 1996. They offer a 400+ page Pre-Season Draft Guide, a Masters List Customizable Cheatsheet MS Excel program, a Master Draft fantasy drafting program, 17 weekly 60+ page in-season newsletters with daily releases. Their FREE services include a constantly updated NFL news "Quick Bits" page (the pioneer of its kind), scouting reports, depth charts, information forums, exclusive fantasy articles written by our staff of experienced fantasy writers and special features including "Inside the Lines" (offensive lines analysis) and "A Fantasy Mastermind Moment" (special fantasy articles featured at SI.com). Fantasy Sports Online for Dummies says FFMastermind.com contains everything imaginable.

You will have no regrets purchasing this site. Great Value!

9.3 - NON-STANDARD GAMES

FFTOC.com

FFTOC – Fantasy Football Tournament of Champions is a different way to play the game without the possible disadvantages of a draft. You can have any player you choose and this type of play is sweeping the fantasy football world. They fill up very quickly and 2006 will be their third year in existence. Do not walk but run to this site.

I'll be playing this game…under the team name Myrandia Me-ows.

LOTS OF GAMES! LOTS OF WAYS TO WIN!

SportDogGames.com (*New for 2006 Fantasy Football Season*)
SportDog Games has truly unleashed fantasy sports like never before! They have created a new way to play fantasy games! If you're not afraid of change, you're going to want to check out SportDog's fantasy game called Challenge! Their game takes fantasy play right down to its purest level of fantasy. Challenge provides a method of head-to-head drafting that will take place each and every week of the season. The game uses a unique drafting method call, "The Quiver System!" This game will Challenge you every week! With Challenge, there is no more "luck of the draw", no more waiver wire restrictions, no more salary cap issues and most of all, **no more excuses**! It's time to be challenged!

9.4 - FANTASY LEAGUES

PaydaySports.com
One site and many leagues to choose from. Low to very high entry fees. A game to fit every budget. They have a goal of becoming the first site to offer a one million dollar grand prize. Look seriously at Payday sports.

Mock Drafts
  Keep track of which round players are being drafted.
  MockDraftCentral.com
  AntSports.com
  MyFantasyLeague.com
  XpertSports.com
  FantasySharks.com

9.5 - FANTASY FOOTBALL TOOLS

FantasyFootballStarters.com

Work smarter, not harder is the mantra of this site's users. Why spend hours second-guessing your fantasy football draft picks, trades and weekly line-up? From beginner to expert, this is your source of personalized, expert fantasy football advice based on their proven Power Analyzer Products, which have a 70% winning percentage against other so-called "expert" sources. Simply plug in your lineup and their tool does the rest. Let them crunch the numbers...you crush the competition.

FSDashboard.com

FSDashboard is an all encompassing tool that allows you to manage all your fantasy sports teams on one web site. Access your fantasy sports teams via our web site, wireless mobile device, or home phone. FSDashboard is the best way to manage all your fantasy sports teams and get information from multiple sources all in one place. Save time and money with our automation features, profile settings, RSS feeds, and much much more. Become more than just a fantasy player with FSDashboard." Special discount only for purchasers of this book.

Receive a 50% discount off of the first two months of service if they enter the promotion code - DOMINATE.

OnBoardStats.com

OnBoard Stats is a system that shows live scoring fantasy stats on a personal scoreboard. The device is an LED screen that can be placed next to a TV or in a common area. It allows you freedom from your computer but still access to your fantasy team while enjoying the game. This is a fantastic way to see how your team is doing...live...without going to your computer.

FantasyDispute.com

Finally, a web site that resolves fantasy sports disputes in a fair, quick, and inexpensive way. Neutral fantasy experts rule on the propriety of trades or any other league dispute. Keeps the integrity of your league at its highest by using an outside expert to handle disputes between team owners or disputes involving your commissioner.

FantasyFreakinFootball.com

Fantasy Freakin' Football hosts a weekly "Podcast" available through the site and is currently a free service run by Garret Mathany, Bobby Brimmer and Jules McLean. Both Garret and Jules compete annually and have enjoyed financial success in the highly competitive World Championship of Fantasy Football (WCOFF), and the National Fantasy Football Championship (NFFC). Garret Mathany is in the WCOFF Hall of Fame and has won over 30K in Fantasy Football contests. FantasyFreakinFootball.com prides itself on their weekly player projections and having the inside track on which players to keep an eye on. This site is tailored more for the serious Fantasy Football player, but beginners are always welcome.

BrunosDraftKits.com

If you have a live draft with your local friends and need a system to help you track the draft, look no more. Bruno's draft kits were created with the goal of making life easier for the fantasy Commissioner. From their larger pre-printed player labels, to our download and print yourself kits (for last minute needs), to our update sheet that ensures you have an up to date player pool, we go the extra mile to make your life easier on draft night.

MaximumFantasySports.com

Maximum Fantasy Sports is bringing new life to the hard core fantasy football player. They are offering options not found on any other site, such as in-game player changes, multi-team trades and true intelligence within the Auto draft engine. Maximum Fantasy Sports aims to deliver a high quality fantasy experience mixed with entertainment and humor. As a commissioner, you will be able to configure options to customize your league to your desired settings. As a team owner, you'll have unprecedented flexibility in establishing and changing your weekly player lineup.

We understand the limitations of many fantasy sports sites and plan to provide those missing features for you.

9.6 - SITES, SITES, AND MORE SITES

The following sites are categorized by theme, but in no particular order. My apologies for any inadvertent errors.

NFL.com

Everyone probably knows about this site. I would not use it for any advice whatsoever but it is fun to watch all the games and your favorite players rack up the points on Sunday. Almost better than watching live TV.

Yahoo, ESPN, CBS SportsLine.

The big three for fantasy football contests.

Advice Web Sites

FantasyDraftEdge.com

FantasySportsCentral.com

InsiderFootball.com

FootballDiehards.com

NFLFreaks.com

FootballDocs.com

FFToday.com

FantasyIndex.com

FantasyFootballAdvisor.com

CoachBox.com

ProFantasySports.com

MonsterDraft.com

ZarbackReports.com

RotoWire.com

F2FA.com

FootballInjuries.com

FFToolbox.com

DoghouseFootball.com

GridironGrumblings.com

FFSpiral.com

FantasyFootball.com

DraftSharks.com

DRFootball.com

Sandbox.com

4for4.com

FantasySharks.com

AskTheCommish.com

XpertSports.com

FFLPros.com

FantasyFootballXtreme.com

GroganSports.com

FantasyTailgate.com

FantasyFootballCafe.com

FantasyFootballAdvisor.com

Gridiron-Guru.com

KFFL.com

TheFantasyFootballTimes.com

DRFantasyFootball.com

JunkyardJake.com

TheCoachsClipboard.com

FantasyFootballGoldenBoy.com

DominateYourLeague.com

TheFantasyPoint.com

TwoMinuteWarning.com

Money Leagues

PSChallenge.com
Dynasty.EFSports.com
FantasySportzGames.com
CFSLSports.com
HomegrownSports.com
HeySportsFans.com
FantasyFootballLeagues.net
FSRU.com
AZFantasyFootball.com
FFLeagues.com
Fantaball.com
PhenomsFF.com

XpertSports.com
SportsBuff.com
AntSports.com
Head2Head.com
KFFL.com
USFantasySports.com
CDMSports.com
FantasyHeadquarters.com
GLFFL.net
ArrowFantasySports.com
FantasyJungle.com

High Stakes Leagues

WCOFF.com
AFFL.com
FantasyFootballChampionship.com

UFFCLive.com
PaydaySports.com
FantasyVIPs.com

Set Up Your Own Leagues

XpertSports.com
FantasyLeague.com
FFLM.com
StatsWorld.com
FootballSoftware.com
RTSports.com
FBall.com
FantasySports.com
FantasyBowl.com
Net-Commish.com
FleaFlicker.com

FantasySharks.com
FantasyInsights.com
FFLCommish.com
FantasyFootball.StatsWiz.com
FanStar.com
CommissionerOnline.com
TQStats.com
WebLeagueManager.com
FFBManager.com
SonicFantasySports.com

Free Leagues

XpertSports.com
YouthFantasyFootball.com
FleaFlicker.com
Atlantic.CarolinaFantasyFootball.com
FantasyCollegeFootball.Excite.com
FantasyMachine.com
DreamSports.com

FantasySportsUnlimited.com
ForecastFootball.com
SuicideLeague.com
FantasyFootball.StatsWiz.com
MoSneaky.com
HeySportsFans.com
FantasyFootballChallenge.com

CHAPTER 10

A 21 TEAM SALUTE:
The Stats Are Where It's At

WHAT YOU WILL LEARN:

1. The Untold Story / Three Strikes and You're Out
2. What it really comes down to
3. The odds of top ten repeats

Overview

I have broken down my 21 leagues at CBS SportsLine®, which includes 252 teams, and over 3,500 games. Although it is a fraction of the millions of fantasy football games played today, I believe it to be representative of the overall industry. I would add here what I stated earlier, that most fantasy football players have no "real strategy", they only have ideas. So this data is not influenced by team's strategies. It is influenced, however, by player injuries and similar NFL variables. You could be justified in adjusting the final percentage by ten percent higher or lower to include the strategies of the sharks and whales in these leagues.

> **The results are directional. If you spend thousands of dollars creating a statistically accurate sampling, the results would most likely be very similar.**

Some say that hindsight is 20/20. You are about to see some things that will shock you and no one has ever told you before. The key is to understand it. If you understand this information, you will understand better how the game is to be played. If you do not like stats, then please read the words. Most strategies have their basis from this chapter, one way or another.

10.1 - THREE STRIKES AND YOU'RE OUT

All of your fantasy football strategies can be thrown out the window if you do not understand the following three strikes. Your success depends on this.

Now that is what I call a change-up.

Strike 1 - A Bad Draft Hole

Are you playing even up? If you play with twelve coaches evenly matched with no strategies whatsoever, you will find your chances to make the playoffs would be equal, which would translate to 8.3% (1 out of 12). The fact that four teams will make the playoffs does not change this number.

In my 21 teams, with four making the playoffs per league, you would have 84 teams. Now look at what draft hole those four drafted from. Common sense would tell us that each hole would garner 8.3% of the playoff-bound teams, or almost seven teams each. It could vary a bit because of the tainted sample provided, but the final results are more than just a bit off. Let's look at this:

Playoff Draft Holes

DRAFT HOLE	# OF PLAYOFF TEAMS	% GARNERED
1	10	11.9%
2	10	11.9%
3	10	11.9%
4	9	10.7%
5	8	9.5%
6	10	11.9%
7	6	7.1%
8	4	4.8%
9	4	4.8%
10	5	6.0%
11	5	6.0%
12	3	3.6%

Wow, did you notice if you draft in the bottom six holes, your chances of making the playoffs go down dramatically. In fact, the top six positions will get 67.9% of the playoffs, while the bottom six is left with 32.1%. That is a 2 to 1 advantage. A dirty little secret that leagues don't mention.

This means the average player drafting from the bottom six is in a "hole" (excuse the pun) that will be very hard to climb out of. But, because of your strategies, you can overcome the unlucky draw and, if you draw from the top, you will be almost untouchable. Drafting from the bottom is strike one and, just like baseball, three strikes and you're out.

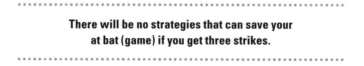

There will be no strategies that can save your at bat (game) if you get three strikes.

The next two strikes have to do with having a good or bad draft and being active or not active on the waiver wire.

Strike 2 - A Bad Draft Grade

You learned in Chapters 4 and 5 how to properly execute your draft. There is no reason, with proper diligence, that you should have a bad draft. However, for this chapter, we have graded each team on draft day by a computer program (the Draft Dominator®). The program did this numerically and then broke it down to a letter grade with "A" being the best, "E" being the worst, and "C" being average. This was only compared to every coach in its own league. No outside influences were used as that might introduce a curve to the grading scale. Each league had three groups…Excellent, Average, Bad.

Strike 3 - Waiver Waver

For the third strike, I looked at the waiver wire (Chapter 6) and broke down activity only. Qualities of the choices were not examined. This also was broken down into three groups. The four most active teams (out of 12) were labeled "top", the bottom four teams were labeled "bottom" and the middle four teams were labeled "mid".

I also included any team that had eight wins or more in their 14 game regular season, because teams with eight wins or more have a very good chance of making the playoffs. I am only talking making the playoffs here, not the championship game.

In the test of 252 teams, there were 116 teams that had eight wins or more (46%). Seventy-two of those teams came from the top six (57.1%) and forty-four teams from the bottom six draft holes (34.9%).

Dig a Little Deeper

To recap, we have our three strikes and you're out rule, which is: A bad hole, a bad draft grade, and waiver waver. But, if you look at the following charts we can break these down further.

#1 - Ignoring the draft hole and the waiver wire activity:

PER 252 TEAMS	#	> 8 WINS	%
All having an excellent draft	110	66	60%
All having an average draft	73	28	38.4%
All having a bad draft	69	22	31.9%

The projected points comes out to about an 8-10 point difference from an excellent draft to a bad draft. But, as you can see, you have a tremendous advantage if you start out with a good draft (60% vs 38.4% vs 31.9%)

#2 - Consider the waiver activity:

PER 252 TEAMS	#	> 8 WINS	%
Top 1/3 in waiver activity	88	52	59.1%
Mid 1/3 in waiver activity	79	38	48.1%
Bottom 1/3 in waiver activity	85	26	30.6%

The numbers are fairly similar to having a good draft. Being in the top for waiver wire activity is a huge advantage. The advantage comes mostly from improving your team.

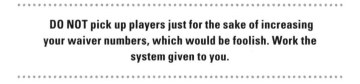

DO NOT pick up players just for the sake of increasing your waiver numbers, which would be foolish. Work the system given to you.

#3 - Splitting the draft hole and only look at the draft. Waiver wire is ignored.

PER 252 TEAMS	#	> 8 WINS	%
Top holes, excellent draft	64	44	68.8%
Bottom holes, excellent draft	46	22	47.8%
Top holes, average draft	41	18	43.9%
Bottom holes, average draft	32	10	31.3%
Top holes, bad draft	21	10	47.6%
Bottom holes, bad draft	48	12	25.0%

Interesting...Did you notice you could have a bad draft from the top holes and your odds are just as good as the coach that had an excellent draft from the bottom holes? In fact, if you draft from the top, you don't have to be that good at your drafting skills but, if you draft from the bottom, you need to be very good.

Now let's take a look at my 21 teams for comparison's sake. I was always in the top 1/3 of my waiver except for one team. I only had two average drafts, the other 19 were excellent (practiced from every hole). However, with my 21 teams, I had 12 in the bottom holes and 9 on the top holes.

PER 252 TEAMS	#	> 8 WINS	%
Top hole, excellent draft	8	5	62.5%
Top hole, average draft	1	0	0.0%
Bottom hole, excellent draft	11	10	90.9%
Bottom hole, average draft	1	0	0.0%

This sampling is too small and only one player, but I wanted to show that you can indeed overcome drafting from the bottom holes and dominate.

#4 - Waiver Activity.
The draft hole will be considered, but not the grade of the draft.

PER 252 TEAMS	#	> 8 WINS	%
Top hole, top 1/3 waiver activity	46	29	63.0%
Bottom hole, top 1/3 waiver activity	42	23	54.8%
Top hole, mid 1/3 waiver activity	36	25	69.4%
Bottom hole, mid 1/3 waiver activity	43	13	30.2%
Top hole, bottom 1/3 waiver activity	44	18	40.9%
Bottom hole, bottom 1/3 waiver act.	41	8	19.5%

The top hole is absolutely an advantage, as demonstrated before, but if you do smart waiver wire work to improve your team, you will be OK. If you ignore your waiver wire responsibilities, go get your crying towel because you will need it.

We have looked at:
1. All draft holes alone
2. All drafts alone
3. All waiver wire activity alone
4. The draft holes, with draft grading
5. The draft holes, with waiver activity

Maybe you want to take this exercise further and match top draft holes with bad draft grades with middle-third waiver activity. Be my guest. The combinations almost seem endless. You can use the chart on the next page, as that is where I got the data from. One last point…if everything went right - top hole, excellent draft, and top-third waiver activity - you would have a 75% chance at eight wins. If everything went wrong and you drafted out of the lower hole, had a bad draft, and did not take care of the waiver wire, your chances would diminish to 16%.

3 STRIKES AND YOU'RE OUT!					
Strike 1	Strike 2	Strike 3			
DRAFT HOLE	DRAFT GRADE	WAIVER ACTIVITY	TEAMS QUALIFIED	TEAMS WITH 8 OR MORE WINS	%
TOP-6	EXCELLENT	TOP	28	21	75.0%
TOP-6	AVG	TOP	12	6	50.0%
TOP-6	BAD	TOP	6	2	33.3%
TOP-6	EXCELLENT	MID	13	11	84.6%
TOP-6	EXCELLENT	BOTTOM	23	12	52.2%
TOP-6	AVG	MID	16	9	56.3%
TOP-6	AVG	BOTTOM	13	3	23.1%
TOP-6	BAD	MID	7	5	**71.4%
TOP-6	BAD	BOTTOM	8	3	37.5%
		TOTAL	126	72	57.1%
BOTTOM-6	BAD	TOP	8	3	37.5%
BOTTOM-6	EXCELLENT	MID	15	4	26.7%
BOTTOM-6	EXCELLENT	BOTTOM	7	2	28.6%
BOTTOM-6	AVG	MID	13	4	30.8%
BOTTOM-6	AVG	BOTTOM	9	2	22.2%
BOTTOM-6	BAD	MID	15	5	33.3%
BOTTOM-6	BAD	BOTTOM	25	4	16.0%
		TOTAL	92	24	26.1%

** I would say that this is an aberration.

10.2 - IT COMES DOWN TO THE POINTS

You have just read about climbing to eight wins and not striking out. Now, we need to look at the game from a point-scoring angle. The first way is to see what the teams that have eight wins or more are scoring. Only look at the 14 regular season weeks. Just as in the NFL, you need to beat the teams who you are suppose to win against. In order for that to happen, you need to have an average score better than 78 points. To keep competitive with the playoff-bound teams, you need to average 91 points.

LEAGUE	AVG SCORE 8 WINS OR BETTER	AVG SCORE LESS THAN 8 WINS
1. Contenders	93.5	73.0
2. Labor Day Celebrations	88.6	78.3
3. Walk the Talk	89.1	77.5
4. VIP Football	88.9	79.0
5. Black & Blue Division	85.9	80.5
6. Horse Traders Wanted	94.0	78.9
7. The Gridiron Classic	90.4	79.6
8. Lonely Hearts Club Band	90.5	74.7
9. Survivor	88.1	75.4
10. Who has Their Shi?	91.8	76.0
11. Double Down	92.0	73.9
12. Colonel Mustards Misfits	87.7	76.4
13. Deal & Play	89.1	72.8
14. For the Real Fan	92.2	80.9
15. Men are from Mars	91.7	78.3
16. Prime Time Football	88.7	80.0
17. West Coast Football	92.1	74.7
18. BS	92.3	73.6
19. NFL 2KV	92.2	80.4
20. The Big Dawgs	88.8	82.4
21. The Money Shot	91.5	76.2
AVERAGE	**90.4**	**77.3**

My 21 teams averaged 95.5 points over the regular season.

For another point of view, compare the various teams from the first seven weeks of the season until the last seven weeks. This excludes the playoff and championship game. What we are looking for is improvement of your team. This next chart proves most fantasy football players are only looking to "play the next game" and does not have a clue on how to make steady improvement.

There are three groups:
1. All - every team in that league (12)
2. Winners – every team that won for that week
   (not the teams with eight or more wins).
   Even bad teams can score high for any particular week.
3. My team, listed by name

My goal was to be above the average "All" score in the first seven weeks and then blow past the "Winners" average in the last seven weeks. The main point was to improve as the year went on. Let's see how I did.

League Improvement Chart

LEAGUE NAME	FIRST 7 WKS	LAST 7 WKS	% IMPROVED
1. Contenders			
All	83.1	83.6	.6%
Winners	94.8	97.8	3.0%
Atomizers	87.1	100.5	13.3%
2. Labor Day Celebrations			
All	82.4	84.3	2.2%
Winners	92.0	95.5	3.6%
Cheese Heads	90.8	93.7	3.1%
3. Walk the Talk			
All	82.4	82.8	.5%
Winners	93.9	95.0	1.1%
Daffy	68.7	109.5	37.3%
4. VIP Football			
All	83.4	84.6	1.4%
Winners	94.0	97.1	3.2%
Geronimo	90.0	97.4	7.6%
3. Black & Blue Division			
All	82.6	83.9	1.6%
Winners	95.5	96.6	1.1%
Gold Stars	77.6	102.7	24.4%

4. Horse Traders Wanted

All	84.5	85.8	1.6%
Winners	95.0	99.9	4.9%
Hang'em High	97.4	127.8	23.8%

5. The Gridiron Classic

All	84.5	83.7	-1.0%
Winners	94.5	97.5	3.1%
Hellcat Cool	90.4	109.2	17.2%

6. Lonely Hearts Club Band

All	83.5	81.8	-2.1%
Winners	95.2	96.4	1.2%
Joker	92.8	112.2	17.3%

7. Survivor

All	82.9	82.7	-.3%
Winners	94.6	96.2	1.7%
Lionheart	90.8	110.5	17.8%

10. Who has Their Shi?

All	82.4	82.8	.5%
Winners	92.9	97.6	4.9%
Lotta Bull	87.7	102.8	14.7%

11. Double Down

All	83.0	83.0	0.0%
Winners	95.1	95.9	.8%
Lupas	93.0	107.8	13.7%

12. Colonel Mustards Misfits

All	83.2	82.8	-.5%
Winners	95.5	93.6	-2.0%
Mexican Mudcats	88.0	111.7	21.2%

13. Deal & Play

All	83.1	78.7	-5.6%
Winners	97.1	93.0	-4.4%
Nemo	78.2	83.1	5.9%

14. For the Real Fan

All	83.9	87.3	3.9%
Winners	94.7	98.0	3.4%
Pistola Pete	86.4	95.3	9.3%

15. Men are from Mars

All	83.4	84.3	1.2%
Winners	95.3	96.6	1.4%
Pooh	89.3	116.5	23.3%

16. Prime Time Football

All	83.5	83.8	.4%
Winners	95.8	95.1	-.7%
Rachael's Robins	90.8	84.1	-8.0%

17. West Coast Football

All	82.0	81.9	-.2%
Winners	93.0	93.9	1.0%
Ramblin Man	81.1	108.2	25.0%

18. BS

All	80.7	82.1	1.7%
Winners	94.0	97.0	3.1%
Rocket Man	84.1	103.6	18.8%

19. NFL 2KV

All	85.2	83.5	-2.1%
Winners	97.3	94.5	-2.9%
Tweety	79.1	104.4	24.2%

20. The Big Dawgs

All	84.1	85.8	2.0%
Winners	96.7	97.7	1.0%
Wanna Bees	93.1	100.1	7.0%

21. The Money Shot

All	83.0	82.2	-1.0%
Winners	94.1	93.5	-.6%
Zero Zippos	93.5	112.3	16.7%

Over the 14 game season, all 12 teams as a league ("All" category) improved an average of just .2%. The "Winners" scores improved an average of 1.6%. The serpentine draft purposely makes teams start out evenly. Your job is to improve as the season goes on. My teams improved an average of 15.9%. That is like having an extra player on my roster. I was ready for the championship game because that is what I set out to do on draft day.

Staying with the point themes, you learned (in section 8.5) that the average margin of victory was 24.3 points per game. This alone tells you that a kicker or a tight end who averages four points per game is not going to greatly affect your team's chances. Take advantage of this opportunity:

The chances of you winning or losing by 5 points or less is 15%.

The chances of you winning or losing between 6 to 15 points are 54.9%.

The chances of you winning or losing by 16 or more points are 30.1%.

This emphasizes the situation that if you must play a kicker or TE who is on a bye week, your chance of winning the game is only slightly lowered, as only 15% of the fantasy football games are decided by what that player will average for you or against you.

Do not automatically replace your bye week kicker or TE. Decide if it is smarter to replace or play him from the team concept.

10.3 - WHO WILL RETURN TO THE TOP 10?

Back in Chapter 4, we discussed that many top players do not return to the top ten the next year. It is not who repeats that counts, it is how many repeat. The points are based on the normal performance scoring system and are only a measuring device for the following charts.

Annual Top Ten Repeaters

Quarterbacks

Rank	2000	PTS	x	2001	PTS	x	2002	PTS	x	2003	PTS	x	2004	PTS	x	2005	PTS
1	D CULPEPPER	397		K WARNER	358		R GANNON	343		P MANNING	316	x	P MANNING	451	x	C PALMER	320
2	J GARCIA	391	x	J GARCIA	353	x	D CULPEPPER	310	x	D CULPEPPER	312	x	D CULPEPPER	438		P MANNING	288
3	P MANNING	353	x	B FAVRE	313		P MANNING	310	x	T GREEN	292	x	D MCNABB	342		T BRADY	287
4	R GANNON	342	x	R GANNON	311	x	M VICK	306		M HASSELBECK	292		B FAVRE	311		M HASSELBECK	264
5	D MCNABB	320	x	P MANNING	307	x	T GREEN	304	x	S MCNAIR	281		J PLUMMER	307	x	E MANNING	262
6	M BRUNELL	261		D MCNABB	302		ABROOKS	301	x	B FAVRE	279	x	T GREEN	306		D BREES	248
7	K COLLINS	252		S MCNAIR	301	x	T BRADY	295	x	ABROOKS	270	x	J DELHOMME	306	x	D BLEDSOE	241
8	B FAVRE	236	x	ABROOKS	295	x	D BLEDSOE	290		J KITNA	267		D BREES	295	x	K COLLINS	241
9	D BLEDSOE	223		J FIEDLER	258		S MCNAIR	290	x	B JOHNSON	259		ABROOKS	285		J PLUMMER	241
10	K WARNER	219	x	K STEWART	249		J GARCIA	287		T BRADY	254	x	T BRADY	279	x	J DELHOMME	234
MADE TOP 10 NEXT YR		6			5			6			6			5			4

Running Backs

Rank	2000	PTS	x	2001	PTS	x	2002	PTS	x	2003	PTS	x	2004	PTS	x	2005	PTS
1	M FAULK	371	x	M FAULK	326	x	P HOLMES	369	x	P HOLMES	357	x	S ALEXANDER	291	x	S ALEXANDER	340
2	E JAMES	319		P HOLMES	259	x	R WILLIAMS	304	x	L TOMLINSON	340	x	T BARBER	287	x	L TOMLINSON	305
3	E GEORGE	279		S ALEXANDER	250	x	L TOMLINSON	296	x	A GREEN	322		L TOMLINSON	277	x	T BARBER	293
4	M ANDERSON	246	x	A GREEN	245		C PORTIS	276	x	J LEWIS	282		C MARTIN	268		L JOHNSON	277
5	A GREEN	237	x	C MARTIN	238	x	S ALEXANDER	264	x	C PORTIS	259	x	D DAVIS	247	x	E JAMES	251
6	F TAYLOR	232		C DILLON	220		C GARNER	256		D MCALLISTER	251	x	E JAMES	244	x	L JORDAN	213
7	C GARNER	230		A SMITH	201		D MCALLISTER	253	x	S ALEXANDER	247	x	C DILLON	242	x	R JOHNSON	212
8	C MARTIN	230	x	L TOMLINSON	198	x	T BARBER	241		F TAYLOR	215		R JOHNSON	216		C PORTIS	208
9	T BARBER	219		R WILLIAMS	193		T HENRY	226		R WILLIAMS	213	x	W MCGAHEE	202		M ANDERSON	185
10	S DAVIS	217		D RHODES	174		E GEORGE	221		S DAVIS	201		B WESTBROOK	202		T JONES	182
MADE TOP 10 NEXT YR		3			4			6			2			5			

Dominate Fantasy Football

Annual Top Ten Repeaters

Wide Receivers

	2000	PTS	2001	PTS	2002	PTS	2003	PTS	2004	PTS	2005	PTS
1	R SMITH	221	X M HARRISON	234	X M HARRISON	229	X R MOSS	261	M MUHAMMAD	223	S SMITH	227
2	T OWENS	221	X T OWENS	226	X T OWENS	219	T HOLT	232	X M HARRISON	199	L FITZGERALD	198
3	R MOSS	220	X R SMITH	198	H WARD	218	C JOHNSON	188	J WALKER	196	S MOSS	192
4	M HARRISON	210	D BOSTON	193	X R MOSS	188	X H WARD	178	J HORN	196	X C JOHNSON	190
5	I BRUCE	197	J SMITH	176	A TOOMER	179	D MASON	177	X T OWENS	194	X T HOLT	180
6	D ALEXANDER	192	X R MOSS	176	J HORN	176	A BOLDIN	172	D BENNETT	186	J GALLOWAY	180
7	T HOLT	192	X T HOLT	170	P BURESS	172	S MOSS	172	X T HOLT	186	C CHAMBERS	177
8	T BROWN	179	X T BROWN	167	D DRIVER	170	X M HARRISON	168	R WAYNE	184	A BOLDIN	177
9	J HORN	177	J RICE	166	P PRICE	165	X T OWENS	164	X C JOHNSON	169	X M HARRISON	177
10	A TOOMER	164	D MASON	166	M BOOKER	164	D JACKSON	164	B STOKLEY	165	H WARD	156
MADE TOP 10 NEXT YR	6		3		4		4		3		3	

DEFENSES

	2000	2001	2002	2003	2004	2005
1	RAVENS	X STEELERS	X BUCCANEERS	PATRIOTS	X BILLS	PANTHERS
2	TITANS	BEARS	X EAGLES	RAVENS	STEELERS	X BEARS
3	BUCCANEERS	X EAGLES	X PACKERS	RAMS	X RAVENS	X STEELERS
4	DOLPHINS	PACKERS	PANTHERS	X DOLPHINS	X PATRIOTS	SEAHAWKS
5	SAINTS	X BUCCANEERS	RAIDERS	X BUCCANEERS	REDSKINS	COLTS
6	REDSKINS	RAMS	DOLPHINS	X TITANS	JETS	X BUCCANEERS
7	STEELERS	PATRIOTS	FALCONS	COWBOYS	X BUCCANEERS	X REDSKINS
8	RAIDERS	BROWNS	TITANS	CHIEFS	EAGLES	BRONCOS
9	GIANTS	JETS	X STEELERS	X PANTHERS	BEARS	GIANTS
10	EAGLES	CHARGERS	SAINTS	BILLS	FALCONS	JAGUARS
MADE TOP 10 NEXT YR	3	4	4	4	4	4

Annual Top Ten Repeaters

Kickers

	2000	PTS		2001	PTS		2002	PTS		2003	PTS		2004	PTS		2005	PTS
1	M STOVER	141		J ELAM	130	x	J FEELY	144		J WILKINS	169	x	A VINATIERI	153		J FEELY	154
2	R LONGWELL	137	x	K BROWN	130	x	D AKERS	140		M VANDERJAGT	163	x	J ELAM	133		N RACKERS	152
3	D AKERS	126		J WILKINS	129	x	J CARNEY	136		M STOVER	140		J REED	126	x	S GRAHAM	131
4	M VANDERJAGT	123	x	M VANDERJAGT	127		R LONGWELL	130		J KASAY	131		S GRAHAM	124		L TYNES	129
5	O MARE	119	x	M STOVER	121		S JANIKOWSKI	130		G ANDERSON	125	x	D AKERS	124		J KASAY	127
6	S JANIKOWSKI	114	x	J FEELY	119	x	J ELAM	122		R LONGWELL	122	x	R LONGWELL	122	x	J WILKINS	125
7	S CHRISTIE	111	x	D AKERS	117		M ANDERSON	119	x	J ELAM	122	x	M VANDERJAGT	121	x	M VANDERJAGT	121
8	K BROWN	109		J CARNEY	115	x	A VINATIERI	119		J BROWN	116	x	M STOVER	121		J BROWN	120
9	A VINATIERI	108	x	A VINATIERI	115		O MARE	116		D AKERS	116		R LINDELL	119	x	R LINDELL	119
10	D BRIEN	108		P EDINGER	114		J NEDNEY	113	x	A VINATIERI	114		N KAEDING	116	x	J REED	117
MADE TOP 10 NEXT YR		5			5			5			2			6			4

You'll be lucky if there are five, or 50%. There are many reasons for a player to not repeat the following year; injuries are the leading cause. I would like to reiterate two points. All the so-called experts are correct only 50% of the time; therefore, you need not rely on these rankings as an exact. The second point is you also will make the right choice only 50% of the time. Do not be upset with yourself. There are just too many variables. Remember, all the other coaches are in the same boat.

10.4 - LEAGUE BREAKDOWNS

The following breaks down all my leagues and shows: The draft position, total points scored, team name, drafting grade (starters, overall), waiver wire pickups, free agent pickups, total % pickups for league, players remaining (from game 1 to game 14) and the W-L record. Much of the data for this book was gleaned from this chart. The other team names were "adjusted" to protect the innocent (and the guilty).

League Breakdowns

Gray row indicates playoff teams.
Bold row indicates overall champion.

1. CONTENDERS									# WAIVER WIRE	# ADD/ DROPS	TOT. pickup %		# PLAYERS REMAINING	%
DRAFT POS.	TOT. PTS.	TEAM NAME	RECORD			DRAFT GRADE								
			W	L	T	ST.	O.							
5	1354	SHA	10	4	0	C	C		16	18	12.4%		7	50%
11	**1314**	**ATOMIZERS**	**8**	**6**	**0**	**B**	**B**		**13**	**32**	**16.4%**		**7**	**50%**
2	1270	TEA	8	6	0	B	B		15	13	10.2%		6	43%
8	1089	LAB	5	8	1	B	B		14	10	8.7%		7	50%
6	1437	BUM	11	3	0	A	A		14	21	12.7%		6	43%
1	1149	BIR	8	6	0	A	B		12	8	7.3%		8	57%
9	963	PST	6	8	0	C	C		6	8	5.1%		9	64%
10	832	THU	3	11	0	E	D		3	5	2.9%		10	71%
4	1334	SOL	11	3	0	D	B		11	13	8.7%		7	50%
12	1149	KEY	6	7	1	C	C		3	4	2.5%		9	64%
3	1075	FAM	4	10	0	E	E		12	9	7.6%		6	43%
7	1027	WHO	2	10	2	D	E		10	5	5.5%		7	50%
									129	146	275			53% AVG

2. LABOR DAY CELEBRATIONS

DRAFT POS.	TOT. PTS.	TEAM NAME	RECORD			DRAFT GRADE		# WAIVER WIRE	# ADD/ DROPS	TOT. pickup %	# PLAYERS REMAINING	%
			W	L	T	ST.	O.					
10	1244	OAK	8	6		B	B	8	18	9.8%	7	50%
6	1292	CHEESE HEADS	5	8	1	A	B	16	21	13.9%	5	36%
8	1084	MOU	5	9		E	E	9	5	5.3%	6	43%
9	1042	BAL	5	9		A	E	14	9	8.6%	7	50%
2	1360	SIL	9	5		B	C	13	18	11.7%	6	43%
5	1266	BUD	9	5		B	A	16	16	12.0%	5	36%
1	1214	LAS	9	5		B	B	13	17	11.3%	6	43%
3	1188	O'BO	8	4	2	E	C	3	7	3.8%	8	57%
11	1170	KIC	9	5		A	D	17	11	10.5%	6	43%
7	1134	DEU	6	8		C	D	5	6	4.1%	9	64%
12	990	SAN	5	8	1	B	B	6	8	5.3%	8	57%
4	1033	NW	4	10		C	C	4	6	3.8%	9	64%
								124	142	266		49%
												AVG

3. WALK THE TALK

DRAFT POS.	TOT. PTS.	TEAM NAME	RECORD			DRAFT GRADE		# WAIVER WIRE	# ADD/ DROPS	TOT. pickup %	# PLAYERS REMAINING	%
			W	L	T	ST.	O.					
4	1392	NIK	12	2		A	B	6	12	5.8%	8	57%
7	1167	TIC	8	6		A	A	19	19	12.3%	6	43%
1	1248	DAFFY	7	7		C	C	19	33	16.8%	6	43%
9	948	BOO	5	9		A	B	12	17	9.4%	5	36%
6	1172	COM	8	6		E	D	13	14	8.7%	7	50%
5	1136	DUF	8	6		C	B	7	10	5.5%	8	57%
3	1083	RAV	7	7		C	C	18	8	8.4%	7	50%
10	1127	VOO	5	9		E	E	10	22	10.4%	7	50%
2	1373	WHY	9	5		D	A	6	29	11.3%	9	64%
11	1092	BIR	7	7		D	D	5	10	4.9%	10	71%
12	1092	LAS	4	10		A	D	3	8	3.6%	6	43%
8	1005	CRU	4	10		C	C	7	2	2.9%	11	79%
								125	184	309		54%
												AVG

Gray row indicates playoff teams.
Bold row indicates overall champion.

4. VIP FOOTBALL

DRAFT POS.	TOT. PTS.	TEAM NAME	RECORD			DRAFT GRADE		# WAIVER WIRE	# ADD/ DROPS	TOT. pickup %	# PLAYERS	% REMAINING
			W	L	T	ST.	O.					
7	**1312**	**GEROMINO**	**9**	**4**	**1**	**B**	**C**	**12**	**43**	**21.7%**	**5**	**36%**
1	1335	BER	7	6	1	A	B	6	1	2.8%	8	57%
8	1082	RAT	6	8		A	A	26	8	13.4%	7	50%
5	1092	AMA	5	9		D	C	9	2	4.3%	10	71%
3	1367	3PE	9	5		C	D	13	6	7.5%	9	64%
9	1092	TAH	8	6		D	D	4	7	4.3%	7	50%
2	1216	DUF	4	9	1	B	B	2	2	1.6%	11	79%
10	975	PAU	3	11		E	D	20	8	11.1%	7	50%
6	1366	STE	10	3	1	B	B	14	1	5.9%	8	57%
4	1197	TRA	10	4		D	C	15	10	9.9%	9	64%
12	1137	BLA	9	5		E	E	12	17	11.5%	4	29%
11	939	LAB	2	12		D	C	1	14	5.9%	9	64%
								134	119	253		56% AVG

5. BLACK & BLUE DIVISION

DRAFT POS.	TOT. PTS.	TEAM NAME	RECORD			DRAFT GRADE		# WAIVER WIRE	# ADD/ DROPS	TOT. pickup %	# PLAYERS	% REMAINING
			W	L	T	ST.	O.					
9	**1262**	**GOLD STARS**	**8**	**6**		**B**	**A**	**11**	**39**	**17.8%**	**9**	**64%**
1	1264	CRA	7	7		B	B	11	9	7.1%	10	71%
5	1031	QUA	5	9		C	B	16	18	12.1%	8	57%
8	1112	FLY	3	11		A	A	3	3	2.1%	11	79%
4	1374	PFS	12	2		D	A	11	11	7.8%	9	64%
7	1260	GO S	8	6		C	C	4	10	5.0%	11	79%
11	1138	SEE	6	8		E	E	13	4	6.0%	8	57%
2	1124	CLO	5	8	1	A	A	24	21	16.0%	6	43%
12	985	FRO	8	5	1	D	E	7	13	7.1%	8	57%
6	1268	BLU	8	6		E	E	6	7	4.6%	5	36%
3	1069	SAF	8	6		E	E	11	9	7.1%	7	50%
10	1092	LAM	5	9		E	C	16	4	7.1%	7	50%
								133	148	281		59% AVG

Gray row indicates playoff teams.
Bold row indicates overall champion.

6. HORSE TRADERS WANTED

DRAFT POS.	TOT. PTS.	TEAM NAME	RECORD W	L	T	DRAFT GRADE ST.	O.	# WAIVER WIRE	# ADD/ DROPS	TOT. pickup %	# PLAYERS REMAINING	% PLAYERS REMAINING
2	1577	HANG EM HIGH	11	3		A	A	11	20	10.9%	5	36%
4	1255	BER	8	6		B	B	4	4	2.8%	10	71%
1	1245	MUL	6	8		D	C	3	2	1.8%	11	79%
11	1111	RHO	6	8		B	B	12	17	10.2%	6	43%
5	1248	FRE	9	5		B	B	7	8	5.3%	8	57%
6	1058	LOZ	6	8		C	B	16	15	10.9%	5	36%
12	1010	PIL	6	8		E	E	13	8	7.4%	3	21%
9	1193	BAL	4	10		A	B	10	2	4.2%	2	14%
3	1359	HEL	9	5		B	A	17	8	8.8%	7	50%
10	1138	TEA	9	5		B	B	26	19	15.8%	3	21%
7	1089	PAR	5	9		D	B	23	19	14.7%	6	43%
8	1030	DAB	5	9		D	D	16	5	7.4%	5	36%
								158	127	285		42% AVG

7. THE GRIDIRON CLASSIC

DRAFT POS.	TOT. PTS.	TEAM NAME	RECORD W	L	T	DRAFT GRADE ST.	O.	# WAIVER WIRE	# ADD/ DROPS	TOT. pickup %	# PLAYERS REMAINING	% PLAYERS REMAINING
4	1398	HELLCAT COOL	11	2	1	B	A	10	21	10.9%	8	57%
8	1145	MHF	6	8		B	A	14	3	6.0%	7	50%
6	1133	THU	6	8		B	C	4	7	3.9%	10	71%
5	1109	BUD	3	11		C	C	20	5	8.8%	3	21%
2	1270	G-M	9	4	1	A	A	26	6	11.2%	8	57%
12	1062	MAN	8	5	1	C	B	11	19	10.5%	5	36%
1	1248	BAN	8	6		A	A	6	4	3.5%	10	71%
11	1212	STR	5	9		E	E	29	12	14.4%	6	43%
3	1351	REA	12	2		B	B	10	7	6.0%	6	43%
10	1174	DOU	7	7		A	A	20	15	12.3%	4	29%
9	1102	ACE	5	8	1	B	E	7	3	3.5%	7	50%
7	925	JAC	2	12		D	A	6	20	9.1%	2	14%
								163	122	285		45% AVG

Gray row indicates playoff teams.
Bold row indicates overall champion.

8. LONEY HEARTS CLUB BAND

DRAFT POS.	TOT. PTS.	TEAM NAME	RECORD			DRAFT GRADE		# WAIVER WIRE	# ADD/ DROPS	TOT. pickup %	# PLAYERS	% REMAINING
			W	L	T	ST.	O.					
6	1436	JOKER	12	2		A	B	11	23	15.5%	8	57%
4	1288	DYN	7	7		A	A	5	5	4.5%	5	36%
11	1064	BEL	7	7		A	B	15	5	9.1%	6	43%
9	848	EL D	1	13		E	C	2	3	2.3%	10	71%
7	1228	BIG	10	4		C	E	5	9	6.4%	10	71%
1	1200	SKI	9	5		B	C	13	10	10.5%	5	36%
2	1277	HOR	8	6		A	B	15	4	8.6%	6	43%
8	1153	TWE	6	8		A	A	8	12	9.1%	8	57%
5	1185	JEF	9	5		C	C	17	16	15.0%	6	43%
3	1278	DAN	8	6		D	D	7	11	8.2%	7	50%
10	1218	VOO	6	8		C	C	12	7	8.6%	7	50%
12	703	STU	1	13		C	D	2	3	2.3%	8	57%
								112	108	220		51% AVG

9. SURVIVOR

DRAFT POS.	TOT. PTS.	TEAM NAME	RECORD			DRAFT GRADE		# WAIVER WIRE	# ADD/ DROPS	TOT. pickup %	# PLAYERS	% REMAINING
			W	L	T	ST.	O.					
8	1410	LIONHEART	9	5		A	A	13	29	15.7%	7	50%
7	1175	RAV	8	6		E	D	18	6	9.0%	6	43%
2	1153	WHE	8	6		A	B	6	8	5.2%	7	50%
5	1094	CAR	4	10		A	A	7	3	3.7%	6	43%
4	1273	JAC	10	4		C	C	10	7	6.4%	6	43%
6	1198	PFS	10	4		C	A	19	18	13.9%	8	57%
3	1084	BAK	5	9		C	D	19	12	11.6%	4	29%
12	994	BX B	3	11		E	D	8	7	5.6%	5	36%
1	1369	BB'S	10	4		C	B	12	2	5.2%	8	57%
9	1060	ROA	10	4		D	E	19	8	10.1%	7	50%
11	1144	MAJ	4	10		E	E	8	10	6.7%	3	21%
10	962	IRI	3	11		E	E	8	10	6.7%	8	57%
								147	120	267		45% AVG

Gray row indicates playoff teams.
Bold row indicates overall champion.

10. WHO HAS IT TOGETHER

DRAFT POS.	TOT. PTS.	TEAM NAME	RECORD			DRAFT GRADE		# WAIVER WIRE	# ADD/ DROPS	TOT. pickup %	# PLAYERS REMAINING	%
			W	L	T	ST.	O.					
3	1437	LOTTA BULL	10	4		B	B	9	18	9.8%	8	57%
1	1264	EYE	9	5		A	A	21	11	11.6%	5	36%
9	1223	STE	9	5		A	B	15	8	8.3%	6	43%
5	883	ZIN	3	10	1	B	B	0	0	0.0%	12	86%
2	1299	EAT	11	3		B	B	18	10	10.1%	6	43%
8	1109	JO	7	6	1	C	C	15	20	12.7%	4	29%
4	1123	WHI	5	8	1	C	C	9	14	8.3%	2	14%
10	1012	POI	4	9	1	E	C	10	2	4.3%	6	43%
6	1206	MIA	9	5		C	B	22	13	12.7%	5	36%
7	1134	BRO	5	7	2	D	E	11	28	14.1%	6	43%
11	1114	HAM	6	8		D	C	10	7	6.2%	7	50%
12	1071	DID	3	11		C	D	4	1	1.8%	10	71%
								144	132	276		46%
												AVG

11. DOUBLE DOWN

DRAFT POS.	TOT. PTS.	TEAM NAME	RECORD			DRAFT GRADE		# WAIVER WIRE	# ADD/ DROPS	TOT. pickup %	# PLAYERS REMAINING	%
			W	L	T	ST.	O.					
6	1500	LUPAS	10	4		B	B	9	23	9.5%	7	50%
8	1304	COL	9	5		C	A	9	5	4.2%	6	43%
10	1132	TEA	8	6		C	B	9	17	7.7%	5	36%
5	1086	COW	6	8		D	D	8	10	5.3%	6	43%
9	1152	DOU	9	4	1	E	C	18	16	10.1%	4	29%
2	1089	HAR	7	7		C	C	10	9	5.6%	5	36%
12	996	EAR	3	10	1	C	B	6	10	4.7%	9	64%
4	971	RED	3	11		C	C	13	13	7.7%	6	43%
1	1416	GAM	9	5		A	A	16	18	10.1%	8	57%
3	1222	TEA	9	5		A	C	13	20	9.8%	7	50%
7	1195	OUT	7	7		C	B	14	43	16.9%	3	21%
11	867	COM	3	11		E	E	18	10	8.3%	7	50%
								143	194	337		43%
												AVG

Gray row indicates playoff teams.
Bold row indicates overall champion.

12. COLONEL MUSTARDS MISFITS

DRAFT POS.	TOT. PTS.	TEAM NAME	RECORD W	L	T	DRAFT GRADE ST.	O.	# WAIVER WIRE	# ADD/ DROPS	TOT. pickup %	# PLAYERS REMAINING	%
4	1398	MUDCATS	10	4		A	A	11	29	10.2%	7	50%
1	1208	FAN	9	5		E	E	8	23	7.9%	4	29%
10	1187	LEE	8	6		B	C	3	8	2.8%	9	64%
8	923	TEA	2	12		A	A	21	25	11.7%	0	0%
9	1221	LAK	10	4		C	D	16	23	9.9%	7	50%
2	1217	COL	8	6		C	C	25	45	17.8%	5	36%
7	1135	NY	8	6		C	D	2	2	1.0%	10	71%
11	1085	MAN	6	8		E	D	5	4	2.3%	8	57%
6	1225	MIS	8	6		E	C	22	35	14.5%	3	21%
12	1169	MAL	7	7		A	B	20	22	10.7%	7	50%
5	1137	LAB	4	10		B	A	2	10	3.1%	9	64%
3	1035	BLI	4	10		B	B	24	8	8.1%	3	21%
								159	234	393		43% AVG

13. DEAL & PLAY

DRAFT POS.	TOT. PTS.	TEAM NAME	RECORD W	L	T	DRAFT GRADE ST.	O.	# WAIVER WIRE	# ADD/ DROPS	TOT. pickup %	# PLAYERS REMAINING	%
2	1491	BAN	11	2	1	C	D	13	7	5.5%	9	64%
8	1287	TRU	5	7	2	C	D	8	11	5.2%	9	64%
10	1130	NEMO	5	9		C	C	22	24	12.6%	7	50%
4	967	LAB	4	9	1	C	D	2	13	4.1%	9	64%
3	1228	HEA	10	4		A	A	25	13	10.4%	5	36%
7	1215	MOT	8	6		C	C	28	34	16.9%		0%
9	1084	ALL	8	6		E	E	45	43	24.0%	6	43%
5	849	SIL	2	12		E	E	0	0	0.0%	14	100%
1	1309	OLD	12	2		B	C	13	16	7.9%	7	50%
12	1154	FIR	8	6		D	E	14	17	8.5%	5	36%
6	1123	LIT	7	7		C	C	15	3	4.9%	6	43%
11	758	TWI	2	12		E	E	0	0	0.0%	14	100%
								185	181	366		54% AVG

Gray row indicates playoff teams.
Bold row indicates overall champion.

14. FOR THE REAL FAN

DRAFT POS.	TOT. PTS.	TEAM NAME	RECORD			DRAFT GRADE		# WAIVER WIRE	# ADD/ DROPS	TOT. pickup %	# PLAYERS REMAINING	%
			W	L	T	ST.	O.					
11	1272	PISTOLA PETE	9	5		B	C	14	40	12.9%	8	57%
5	1270	LOW	7	6	1	C	D	13	23	8.6%	4	29%
1	1155	FEA	5	8	1	E	E	12	10	5.3%	6	43%
6	1011	RET	5	9		C	D	21	14	8.4%	7	50%
4	**1421**	**LAB**	**9**	**4**	**1**	**A**	**A**	**2**	**9**	**2.6%**	**8**	**57%**
9	1293	SDH	9	5		B	A	47	67	27.3%	5	36%
12	1281	RAI	8	6		B	B	7	10	4.1%	7	50%
10	994	PAT	3	11		E	D	11	9	4.8%	7	50%
3	1186	LUL	8	6		D	B	13	14	6.5%	6	43%
2	1230	SAR	7	7		C	C	8	5	3.1%	8	57%
8	1181	RAI	7	7		C	A	15	16	7.4%	5	36%
7	1083	DOO	5	8	1	D	C	11	26	8.9%	7	50%
								174	243	417	AVG	46% AVG

15. MEN ARE FROM MARS

DRAFT POS.	TOT. PTS.	TEAM NAME	RECORD			DRAFT GRADE		# WAIVER WIRE	# ADD/ DROPS	TOT. pickup %	# PLAYERS REMAINING	%
			W	L	T	ST.	O.					
8	**1441**	**POOH**	**10**	**4**		**B**	**B**	**13**	**26**	**9.6%**	**7**	**50%**
1	1313	ORL	9	5		B	B	22	28	12.3%	3	21%
12	1061	DOM	9	5		B	B	23	9	7.8%	6	43%
10	1019	INT	4	10		C	C	18	18	8.8%	5	36%
2	1408	POO	9	5		A	A	8	6	3.4%	9	64%
4	1130	LAS	6	8		A	B	19	24	10.5%	6	43%
6	1066	PIS	5	9		D	D	21	16	9.1%	5	36%
5	976	DOU	4	10		C	D	17	17	8.3%	5	36%
11	1194	SIL	8	6		E	E	8	21	7.1%	6	43%
9	1164	MOT	7	7		D	D	18	34	12.7%	5	36%
7	1123	PLA	7	7		D	E	6	13	4.7%	6	43%
3	1194	GRE	6	8		C	D	14	9	5.6%	9	64%
								187	221	408	AVG	43% AVG

Gray row indicates playoff teams.
Bold row indicates overall champion.

16. PRIME TIME FOOTBALL

DRAFT POS.	TOT. PTS.	TEAM NAME	RECORD			DRAFT GRADE		# WAIVER WIRE	# ADD/ DROPS	TOT. pickup %	# PLAYERS REMAINING	%
			W	L	T	ST.	O.					
3	1343	BAC	9	3	2	A	A	17	13	7.9%	7	50%
8	1225	RACHAELS	7	6	1	B	B	15	46	16.0%	6	43%
11	1052	VAL	7	7		C	B	24	12	9.4%	8	57%
1	1090	MAS	4	9	1	B	A	3	9	3.1%	9	64%
4	1187	THU	9	5		D	D	14	12	6.8%	6	43%
7	1181	KJ	9	5		C	C	9	15	6.3%	4	29%
2	1313	BAC	8	5	1	B	B	5	5	2.6%	11	79%
9	1136	P-TO	6	8		D	B	17	26	11.3%	6	43%
10	1188	ABI	8	6		D	D	14	7	5.5%	8	57%
12	1320	MOT	7	7		E	D	10	26	9.4%	8	57%
6	1059	DUS	5	9		C	D	16	19	9.2%	5	36%
5	959	TEA	2	11	1	E	E	14	33	12.3%	4	29%
								158	223	381		49%
												AVG

17. WEST COAST FOOTBALL

DRAFT POS.	TOT. PTS.	TEAM NAME	RECORD			DRAFT GRADE		# WAIVER WIRE	# ADD/ DROPS	TOT. pickup %	# PLAYERS REMAINING	%
			W	L	T	ST.	O.					
12	1326	RAMBLING	10	4		B	A	10	38	20.4%	6	43%
9	1117	FIS	8	6		E	C	3	12	6.4%	8	57%
8	1093	J-S	6	7	1	C	B	4	2	2.6%	8	57%
11	1033	BAD	4	10		C	B	24	3	11.5%	5	36%
3	1400	MOR	10	3	1	C	D	6	19	10.6%	7	50%
1	1272	DEV	8	6		A	D	2	2	1.7%	12	86%
10	1153	FUS	6	6		D	E	11	11	9.4%	5	36%
2	944	WES	2	12		A	A	0	5	2.1%	7	50%
7	1330	WIL	9	5		C	B	11	13	10.2%	5	36%
6	1104	FAT	7	6	1	D	C	10	13	9.8%	6	43%
5	1017	RAM	6	7	1	D	E	19	15	14.5%	7	50%
4	978	LOV	5	9		B	C	0	2	0.9%	7	50%
								100	135	235		49%
												AVG

Gray row indicates playoff teams.
Bold row indicates overall champion.

18. BS

DRAFT POS.	TOT. PTS.	TEAM NAME	RECORD			DRAFT GRADE		# WAIVER WIRE	# ADD/ DROPS	TOT. pickup %	# PLAYERS REMAINING	% PLAYERS REMAINING
			W	L	T	ST.	O.					
7	1048	NEV	8	6		B	B	13	4	5.5%	8	57%
6	1086	CO	6	8		D	E	18	18	11.7%	7	50%
5	1053	TX H	6	8		C	B	18	20	12.4%	5	36%
10	861	ERO	3	11		E	E	9	3	3.9%	8	57%
11	1314	ROCKET	11	3		B	A	16	21	12.1%	8	57%
12	1159	MAS	7	7		C	C	14	18	10.4%	6	43%
8	1082	DOU	5	8	1	C	A	11	12	7.5%	6	43%
9	871	CAN	3	11		E	D	1	4	1.6%	11	79%
4	1490	PUG	11	3		B	A	11	6	5.5%	7	50%
2	1282	FRE	9	5		A	A	18	21	12.7%	6	43%
3	1326	DIS	8	6		D	D	24	12	11.7%	8	57%
1	1101	WIN	6	7	1	C	C	4	11	4.9%	4	29%
								157	150	307		50% AVG

19. NFL 2KV

DRAFT POS.	TOT. PTS.	TEAM NAME	RECORD			DRAFT GRADE		# WAIVER WIRE	# ADD/ DROPS	TOT. pickup %	# PLAYERS REMAINING	% PLAYERS REMAINING
			W	L	T	ST.	O.					
8	1285	TWEETY	8	6		A	A	15	38	16.0%	6	43%
1	1302	BJP	7	7		D	C	12	37	14.8%	6	43%
3	1191	STO	7	7		B	A	3	5	2.4%	8	57%
4	1120	FAB	6	7	1	A	B	13	5	5.4%	6	43%
6	1155	EC	8	5	1	C	A	10	12	6.6%	7	50%
11	1057	BRA	5	8	1	C	B	18	6	7.3%	5	36%
7	1222	TUR	5	9		C	B	16	19	10.6%	7	50%
12	990	ALL	5	9		E	E	2	10	3.6%	9	64%
2	1376	INM	12	2		A	A	11	17	8.5%	8	57%
5	1346	GRE	11	3	1	B	B	11	8	5.7%	5	36%
10	1031	BLA	4	9	1	D	C	21	18	11.8%	4	29%
9	1087	69E	4	10		A	C	13	11	7.3%	6	43%
								145	186	331		46% AVG

Gray row indicates playoff teams.
Bold row indicates overall champion.

Dominate Fantasy Football

20. THE BIG DAWGS

DRAFT POS.	TOT. PTS.	TEAM NAME	RECORD			DRAFT GRADE		# WAIVER WIRE	# ADD/ DROPS	TOT. pickup %	# PLAYERS	% REMAINING
			W	L	T	ST.	O.					
1	1437	MON	11	3		C	E	5	14	5.0%	10	71%
11	1066	CHA	8	6		C	B	27	20	12.5%	3	21%
3	1353	WANNA BEES	7	6	1	A	A	10	36	12.2%	7	50%
7	1026	SHO	3	11		B	C	8	22	8.0%	6	43%
2	1249	TON	10	4		C	D	17	13	8.0%	7	50%
10	1109	BOR	10	4		D	C	8	11	5.0%	7	50%
4	1178	DAI	6	8		C	C	12	12	6.4%	5	36%
9	1103	SEA	5	9		E	E	10	1	2.9%	8	57%
5	1352	TAI	9	5		A	A	14	28	11.1%	6	43%
8	1175	OAT	7	7		D	D	25	9	9.0%	7	50%
6	1200	BOM	5	8	1	B	C	25	22	12.5%	6	43%
12	1040	CRA	2	12		D	D	18	10	7.4%	4	29%
								179	198	377		45% AVG

21. THE MONEY SHOT

DRAFT POS.	TOT. PTS.	TEAM NAME	RECORD			DRAFT GRADE		# WAIVER WIRE	# ADD/ DROPS	TOT. pickup %	# PLAYERS	% REMAINING
			W	L	T	ST.	O.					
3	1334	ROG	9	4	1	C	B	7	9	6.2%	6	43%
7	1069	BEW	7	7		A	A	9	11	7.7%	5	36%
4	1044	CJS	6	8		C	C	6	3	3.5%	5	36%
2	846	DON	1	12	1	B	E	0	0	0.0%	14	100%
1	1190	DEF	9	4	1	C	C	14	12	10.0%	6	43%
5	1138	BAY	8	6		D	B	34	9	16.6%	8	57%
8	1156	BRU	7	7		A	B	15	4	7.3%	8	57%
9	1177	POC	6	8		B	D	11	3	5.4%	8	57%
10	1441	ZERO ZIPPOS	9	5		B	A	10	26	13.9%	9	64%
6	1302	OUT	9	5		C	C	19	6	9.7%	8	57%
11	1134	BLU	6	7	1	E	E	12	12	9.3%	8	57%
12	1041	STO	5	9		D	C	8	19	10.4%	8	57%
								145	114	259		55% AVG

Gray row indicates playoff teams.
Bold row indicates overall champion.

CHAPTER 11

THE TAXMAN COMETH:
Claiming Your Winnings

WHAT YOU WILL LEARN:

1. Options for what do do with your winnings
2. Inside tips with examples
3. Ways of treating fantasy football as a deduction

Overview

If you're reading this chapter because you dominated your fantasy football league and won, congratulations! Now, pay up. By law, you are legally responsible for claiming any fantasy football winnings you receive to the IRS. This chapter will explain the different options you have for claiming your winnings and will help you explore whether or not you should turn this fun hobby into a full-fledged business.

Warning! The information in this chapter is **NOT** to be considered tax advice in any form. The intent is to cover topics and ideas you should discuss with a tax professional who is familiar with your personal financial situation.

11.1 - TAX OPTIONS FOR CLAIMING YOUR WINNINGS

I have been preparing individual taxes for my clients for almost 25 years and my firm currently averages almost 3,000 prepared returns per year. I decided to include a chapter on taxes in this book because I found that the more I won my fantasy football leagues, the more I relied on my tax knowledge.

How you claim your taxes depends on your current tax bracket and where you plan to be in the future. You have two ways to claim your winnings – as miscellaneous income or as self-employed. If you chose miscellaneous income, you will treat your fantasy football winnings as a hobby. If you chose self employed, you will treat your fantasy football income as a business. Both options have advantages and disadvantages. Your job is to find which area is most advantageous for your particular tax situation.

On any winnings greater than $600, you will receive a 1099 form from the company that paid out your winnings.

Let's talk about each option. On the income side, the miscellaneous income will tax you as ordinary income and payment will be set at your current tax bracket. If you decide to use the other method (Schedule C), you'll pay the ordinary tax **and** the self employment tax.

One for me, one for Uncle Sam.

Hmmm...paying one tax on the money **or** two taxes on the same money. Pretty simple so far? Not so fast. You still need to consider the next part of the equation – your expenses. The *amount* of your expenses will ultimately help you determine which tax option you choose.

Here are three expense considerations (on Schedule A) for your first option related to miscellaneous income:

1. You are never allowed to show a net loss – you can deduct only up to the income on the front of 1040
2. If you don't qualify for Schedule A, none of your expenses are deductible
3. The first two percent of your Adjusted Gross Income (AGI) is subtracted from your Schedule A, fantasy football expenses.

The other side of the equation is to subtract your expenses on Schedule C directly against your fantasy football income. This would be subtracted dollar-for-dollar with no limitations whatsoever, and could even take your gross winnings into a net loss.

Now that you know where your expenses fall, you need to calculate your net income from fantasy football. Your net is your total winnings minus all expenses. Estimate your tax bracket for this year and your "realistic" projection for future years. A net loss would indicate an advantage to use a Schedule C as a self-employed person, especially if there were another unrelated self-employed profit on your tax return. If you do a Schedule A, any net gains would dictate using ordinary miscellaneous income to report your winnings.

We need to take this one more step and explain with some examples. Below are three situations to compare based on the winnings and expenses of three different coaches.

OPTION 1   Schedule C as self-employed.

OPTION 2   1040 front page as miscellaneous income with no Schedule A deduction. (Assume the taxpayer does not qualify for Schedule A.)

OPTION 3   1040 front page as misc. income with full Schedule A deduction.

FANTASY FOOTBALL PLAYERS:

	COACH X	COACH Y	COACH Z
Total Winnings	$32,500	$10,500	$1,000
Total Expenses	$ 8,500	$8,500	$8,500
	-----	-----	-----
NET	$24,000	$2,000	<$7,500>

Now that we know the net for each fantasy football player, we will break down the taxes owed. This will be for federal tax only (no state) and we will assume the taxpayer is in the ordinary tax bracket of 25 percent. The self-employment tax will be figured at 13.04 percent.

COACH X - TAXES OWED:

OPTION 1	$9,129.60
OPTION 2	$8,125.00
OPTION 3	$6,000.00

Option 3 would owe the least amount in taxes, so Coach X should choose not to be self-employed.

COACH Y - TAXES OWED:

OPTION 1	$760.80
OPTION 2	$2,625.00
OPTION 3	$500.00

Coach Y would choose option one as self-employed, unless he knew Schedule A was going to work for him for option 3.

COACH Z - TAXES OWED:

OPTION 1	$0*
OPTION 2	$250.00
OPTION 3	$0

*Realizes a savings of $1,875 on his return against other income. Coach Z prefers to be classified as a self-employed Schedule C filer.

As you can see from the above examples, you'll know the best way to file after you have a few numbers to work with your own personal tax situation. **Your choices can cost or save you your hard-earned dollars.** You'll want to work with your professional tax individual and go over all possible scenarios.

Now you need to choose the direction of how you wish to be taxed. Don't delay, as you need to choose today rather than next April when it's too late to make a choice. You can even start one year with one choice and the next year move to the other choice; however, it is much smarter to be consistent and stick to one choice. You absolutely cannot go back and forth each year, just for the tax advantage. You have now broken down the self-employed business route verses the hobby route.

11.2 - HOW TO TREAT FANTASY FOOTBALL INCOME AS A BUSINESS

Most people (and even some professional tax preparers) will advise that you cannot be self-employed in playing fantasy football. The IRS, however, will tell you that, if you treat this as a business, it can be claimed as a business on your tax return. **The key is treating this as a business.**

With the IRS, it comes down to facts and circumstances. The more facts and circumstances you put on your side, the more likely they will legitimately allow the deduction on your Schedule C.

Here are some considerations:

A. The manner in which the taxpayer carries on the activity.

B. The expertise of the taxpayer and the expertise of the advisers he seeks out.

C. The time and effort spent by the taxpayer on the activity. *This does not have to be full time by any means.*

D. Whether or not the taxpayer has a written business plan and updates this annually. *This is where most drop the ball; write down your intended goals.*

E. The taxpayer's history with respect to the activity.

F. The amount of occasional profits, if any.

G. The elements of personal pleasure or recreation. *Fantasy football is fun, no doubt, but who's to say a business can't be fun? Not even the IRS!*

Your strategy, should you elect to go the self-employed route, is to show the IRS that even though there is personal pleasure involved in fantasy football, you're treating this as a for-profit business. Here are some ideas on how to do so:

1. Open a checking account just for this business and run all income and expenses through this account.

2. Document the time you spend on it. I realize this may be time consuming, but it proves to the IRS the amount of time you've

invested. The more time you can show, the less proof they have that you are purely having fun. *Can you document time in March, when football season is not even near?*

3. Write a business plan. It can be simple, but you must show your intended direction and how you plan to be profitable. For example, *I will join three auction leagues for prize money to "learn" how to win and also join four standard leagues with the intention of making $6k.* The following year, *I will join 10 auction leagues and plan to work 15 hrs a week for 16 weeks to win 20k.*

Next year it can be: *The auction league did not work out and I will now pay entry to two championship leagues and three stan dard leagues, where the total prize money is over $200k. I will also increase my advice sites to 25 percent more than last year because, etc., etc.*

But Honey, I am working.

4. Keep the records of any expertise you received in the advisement of your business.

5. If you were to win in every one of your leagues, what would be the total prize money? You can use the *total* amount to show the IRS the profit intent. Make sure you clip any proof and store it in your file. *Everyone knows you can't win them all, but the IRS must assume your intent is to win them all.*

6. The IRS will state that to claim this as a business, you must show profit two out of five years, and your accountant may agree. The truth is, as long as you are considered a business and you are intending to make a profit, there are no limits to the number of years you can show a loss. However, following my strategies outlined in this book, you should definitely look forward to future profits.

If you consider this business legitimate and treat it as such, the IRS will also see it as legitimate. The bottom line is you are going to win money and you want to legally pay the least amount required.

You may be surprised at all the deductions that could pop up. For example, you can deduct miles driven to the store to pick up your fantasy football magazine, the NFL Sunday ticket for research, part of your monthly Internet expense and even your trip to Vegas to play in the WCOFF, with all travel, lodging and food deductible.

11.3 - HOW TO TREAT FANTASY FOOTBALL INCOME AS A HOBBY

Nothing. Nada. It's that simple. My best advice is to work with your tax professional and use the IRS rules in a legal manner to determine the best option for you.

TEAM(S) DIARY

Use this information that you gather currently to know what to do next year. Look to your leagues tendencies, and build a history of the game itself. You may want to build your own sheet for each team. Below are some of the questions to ask yourself and you might have some of your own. Most of the focus is on RBs but you will need to look at other positions as well.

Questions:

1. How many RBs were injured during the pre-season?
2. Was dropping a kicker during pre-season viable?
3. Were there any surprise players coming out of pre-season?
4. How did the "guarantee" part of the draft work out?
5. Was the draft looser during the early part of the preseason?
6. Do I see any Homerism by the other coaches?
7. How many RBs are injured in the first half of the season as compared to the second half?
8. Do I see any bye trading opportunities coming up?
9. Did my team scores improve from the first 7 games to the last 7 games?
10. How many spots could a coach climb up the waiver wire?
11. When did the player pool handcuffs start disappearing?
12. How often did I use a spotter?
13. By week 10, how often did my team have the most RBs in the league?
14. What week did the waiver wire activity slow down?
15. How many games were won or lost by less than 5 points?
16. _____
17. _____
18. _____
19. _____
20. How many championship games did I win?

WEEKLY DIARY

Team _____

League_____

PRE-SEASON WEEK 1:

PRE-SEASON WEEK 2:

PRE-SEASON WEEK 3:

PRE-SEASON WEEK 4:

WEEK 1:

WEEK 2:

WEEK 3:

WEEK 4:

WEEK 5:

WEEK 6:

WEEK 7:

WEEK 8:

WEEK 9:

WEEK 10:

WEEK 11:

WEEK 12:

WEEK 13:

WEEK 14:

WEEK 15:

WEEK 16: CHAMPIONSHIP

REFERENCE KEY AND NOTES

CHAPTER 2 - BEGINNER'S PARADISE

SEC._____

SEC._____

SEC._____

SEC._____

CHAPTER 3 - SETTING THE BAR

SEC._____

SEC._____

SEC._____

SEC._____

CHAPTER 4 - WELCOME TO TRAINING CAMP

    SEC._____

    SEC._____

    SEC._____

    SEC._____

CHAPTER 5 - THE WAR ROOM

    SEC._____

    SEC._____

    SEC._____

    SEC._____

APPENDIX

CHAPTER 6 - WAIVER WIRE WARRIOR

SEC._____

SEC._____

SEC._____

SEC._____

CHAPTER 7 - THE TRADING DESK

SEC._____

SEC._____

SEC._____

SEC._____

CHAPTER 8 - THE LITTLE THINGS COUNT

SEC._____

SEC._____

SEC._____

SEC._____

CHAPTER 9 - CAN'T GET ENOUGH INFORMATION

SEC._____

SEC._____

SEC._____

SEC._____

APPENDIX

CHAPTER 10 - THE 21 TEAM SALUTE

SEC._____

SEC._____

SEC._____

SEC._____

CHAPTER 11 - THE TAX MAN COMETH

SEC._____

SEC._____

SEC._____

SEC._____

ADDITIONAL NOTES:

TAKE ME TO THE MOVIES

Now that your mind is chock-full of strategies and numbers, you may need a bit of inspiration for the season and there is nothing like a football movie to get your game face on. Below is a list of some of the best ever produced. So grab yourself a cold beverage and some hot popcorn!

Friday Night Lights (2004):

Billy Bob Thornton stars as the coach of the cult-like Permian Panthers at Ratliff Stadium, the largest high school football stadium in the country. Even if you aren't a football fan you'll identify with the themes and values of this story.

Remember the Titans (2000):

In this film, based on a true story, Denzel Washington plays Herman Boone, a black coach of a Virginia high school football team just after the desegregation of the early '70s. As the movie progresses, the players cautiously join together to work as a team.

Any Given Sunday (1999):

This is a hard-hitting look at professional football with Al Pacino as a fading head coach of a Miami football team. He is at odds with the team's owner, played by Cameron Diaz, as well as Jamie Foxx as quarterback.

Rudy (1993):

If you haven't seen this movie, you must not have a television. It's on every other day. (Though my wife cringes, I watch it every chance I get. It's one of my favorites.) Based on a true story, Daniel " Rudy" Ruettiger, played by Sean Astin (Sam on Lord of the Rings), is a working-class kid who dreams of playing football for the University of Notre Dame. Through much adversity and perseverance, he makes it onto the team and a big finish.

Everybody's All-American (1988):

Dennis Quaid and Jessica Lange play a college football star and his wife. The movie follows his life into the pros with the Washington Redskins, and his eventual decline.

North Dallas Forty (1979):

This movie, starring Nick Nolte as a has-been football hero, delves into drug use, violence and sex, not to mention corporate greed and mistreatment of players.

The Longest Yard (1974):

Burt Reynolds stars as a former football star, now in prison, who organizes his fellow inmates into a football team to play against the prison guards. The warden, played by Eddie Albert, then tries to force him to throw the game.

Brian's Song (1971):

Another one based on a true story, this movie chronicles the remarkable friendship between two Chicago Bears roommates and their wives. One, Brian Piccolo is white; the other, Gale Sayers, is black. Get out the hankies when Piccolo learns he is dying of cancer.

Paper Lion (1968):

Based on writer George Plimpton's 1963 tryout for third string quarterback for the Detroit Lions. Alan Alda stars as the football-inept Mr. Plimpton. You can also catch Lion's player Alex Karras and many other Lions of the '60s playing themselves. The coaches were in on the real life stunt, but the players were not.

Knute Rockne: All-American (1940):

Ronald Reagan plays George "the Gipp" Gipper, a dying University of Notre Dame football star. Pat O'Brien plays legendary coach Knute Rockne. Yep, this is where "win one for the Gipper" came from.

About the Author

Randy Giminez, CFP, ChFC, CLU, has owned both a tax business and a financial planning business for 20-plus years located in Hillsdale, MI. He is rated "expert" in chess through the US Chess Federation. He now lives in Blue Springs, MO with his wife and dog.

You can find Randy's fantasy football experience in Chapter 1.

My hope is that this book will help you Dominate your Leagues for years to come.

If you want to share your insights with other readers, I would appreciate your testimonial or review on our site. Please go to www.dominatefantasyfootball.com and add your name to our list of future Dominators.

Thank you for reading this book.